TEACHING CHILDREN A POSITIVE GROWTH MINDSET

A GUIDE TO MODERN TECHNIQUES FOR POSITIVE PARENTING

BY: DANIEL ALEXANDER

© **Copyright Daniel Alexander 2021 - All rights reserved.**

The content contained within this book may not be reproduced, duplicated, or transmitted without direct written permission from the author or the publisher.

Under no circumstances will any blame or legal responsibility be held against the publisher, or author, for any damages, reparation, or monetary loss due to the information contained within this book, either directly or indirectly.

Legal Notice:

This book is copyright protected. It is only for personal use. You cannot amend, distribute, sell, use, quote, or paraphrase any part, or the content within this book, without the consent of the author or publisher.

Disclaimer Notice:

Please note the information contained within this document is for educational and entertainment purposes only. All effort has been executed to present accurate, up-to-date, reliable, complete information. However, no warranties of any kind are declared or implied. Readers acknowledge that the author is not rendering legal, financial, medical, or professional advice. The content within this book has been derived from various sources. Please consult a licensed professional before attempting any techniques outlined in this book.

By reading this document, the reader agrees that under no circumstances is the author responsible for any losses, direct or indirect, incurred due to the use of the information contained within this document, including, but not limited to, errors, omissions, or inaccuracies.

CONTENTS

Introduction	7
1. THE SCIENCE OF MINDSETS	13
The Importance of Mindsets	13
How the Brain Works	14
How Can Mindsets Be Changed?	17
Common Misconceptions About the Growth Mindset	28
2. GROWTH MINDSET AND EMOTIONAL INTELLIGENCE	33
What is Emotional Intelligence?	33
Emotional Intelligence and a Fixed Mindset	39
Emotional Intelligence and Growth Mindset	42
6 Ways to Teach Your Child Good Emotional Intelligence	43
3. COVID-19 AND THE GROWTH MINDSET	53
Can a Growth Mindset Help Students During the Pandemic?	53
Tips for Helping Your Child Maintain a Growth Mindset in the Time of COVID-19.	55
COVID-19 and Distance Learning	59
4. PARENTS	67
Put Your Growth Mindset Mask on First	68
How to React to Failure	69
Praise and Discipline	72
The Judgment of Children	79

    The Way Parents Judge Themselves   82
    Take the Harder Path   83

5. HOW TO STRENGTHEN GRIT IN OUR CHILDREN   84
    Traits of Mental Toughness or Grit   88
    Strategies for Creating Grit in Children   98

6. DEVELOPING A GROWTH MINDSET WITH TEENS   103
    The Teenage Brain   103
    Growth Mindset Strategies for Teens   105
    How to Make Grittier Teens   110
    Growth Mindset and Teen Stress   116

7. GROWTH MINDSET VS. SPORTS PERFORMANCE   118
    How to Develop a Growth Mindset in Young Athletes   123
    Modern Examples of Athletes with Growth Mindsets   130
    A-Team with a Fixed Mindset   136

8. GROWTH MINDSET IN WORK--CASE STUDIES   138

9. A TOOL KIT FOR PARENTS   146
    Courses You and Your Child Can Purchase or Download for Free   146
    Books That Are Great Resources   152

Conclusion   155
References   159

A free gift for our readers
7 tips to developing a growth mindset which you can download by visiting our website www.danielalexanderbooks.com or by scanning the QR code below.

INTRODUCTION

As a small child, I saw my mind synonymous with my brain, enclosed in my skull, and therefore could not be "put to" anything.

A few years later, I realized my mind was not my physical grey matter brain but one of the functions of my brain. I then began to understand that my way of thinking was what made anything possible. So I changed my way of thinking to make the things I wanted to succeed at possible. I did not know then that I was going from a fixed mindset to a growth mindset.

Sadly, I came to this mindset realization on my own. In the 1980's teaching children about the way they think about things and working hard to improve their thoughts was not emphasized as much as simply being smart.

It was a Psychologist named Carol Dweck who began to change this way of thinking. When she was in graduate school, she started researching students who succeeded and students with the same ability levels who were less successful. Through this research, she developed the idea of mindsets. Some people have fixed mindsets, and others have growth mindsets. She published her findings in the book "Mindsets" in 2006.

Now we know a person's mindset is an authentic and vital brain function; however, most parents still struggle with how to help the children around them learn to have a positive mindset that leads to intellectual and positive social growth.

As a school teacher, I taught a wide variety of students over my ten-year career. Many of my students were underprivileged and in the minority. Their mindset was fixed. It was set on defeat and failure. If the school system or my parents or I had implemented some of the information and strategies discussed in the following chapters, my students' outcomes might have been very different.

This book will teach the science of mindsets, what mindsets mean for a person's emotional intelligence, how COVID-19 has affected the mindsets of the world, what parents can do to foster a growth mindset for their children in academics and sports, and how the changes to a teenagers brain affect their mindsets. Some case students are also about how a growth mindset has begun to affect the business world for teens entering the workforce. There will also be a toolkit of reference materials and courses to help parents gather more information.

A few comprehensive studies on mindsets help us understand what we need to do to help our children succeed based on changing brain chemistry through learning and positive mindsets.

Along with the science, I will cover how to change your own or your child's mindset if it needs to be changed. ==There are specific ways to change the way we teach and use praising language.== Some parents and teachers inadvertently reinforce a fixed mindset instead of encouraging the growth mindset because we praise children.

The science of mindsets will also include some tips and courses on how to change a child's mindset before the fixed mindset gets entrenched in their thought process.

There are a few misconceptions about mindsets that need clearing up as well. Like all research, some people interpret the information differently, not in the original study's scope. These misinterpretations have led to people having a "false growth mindset." It has also led to parents and teachers looking for the easy route to a growth mindset. Unfortunately, there is no easy route.

There is a strong correlation between emotional intelligence and a growth mindset. Therefore, your child must have good emotional Intelligence because it helps facilitate and maintain a positive growth mindset.

I will go over tips on how to teach your child to work for the highest level of emotional Intelligence. It will include the emotional intelligence levels and strategies to achieve and maintain a great sense of emotional Intelligence.

Emotional Intelligence and a growth mindset are reciprocal and must be practiced and maintained. There will be a full explanation of what this means.

I explore how the COVID-19 pandemic has influenced people's mindsets. A collective tragedy always affects people in a certain way. The pandemic has led to a different way of learning: outside of the brick-and-mortar school building. I explore ways to use mindset to improve new forms of "distance learning."

Most of Dr. Dweck's research conclusions are geared toward teachers, but there is much advice specifically for parents. Teaching a growth mindset at home is a little different from how it would be taught at school. I go over strategies for parents to use with their children or for themselves in a non-classroom or academic setting.

Grit is another essential aspect of a growth mindset. I will explain the definition of grit and how it can make a person mentally stronger. Grit can equip a child with the mental toughness to help them overcome adversity that is inevitable in life.

A child's brain changes and reconstructs itself when they begin to reach puberty. There are strategies to help parents and teens deal with the difficulties, such as taking risks and the inability to control their impulses. The better parents and teens understand what is happening to the brain, the easier it is to deal with the difficulties that arise for a teenager.

Dr. Dweck does a great job of explaining the difference between the successes and failures of athletes depending on their mindset. Talent is essential to be great at sports, but so is practice and learning to improve. Unfortunately, raw talent can be a double-edged sword for some children who play sports.

The strategies for keeping a grown mindset in sports are a little different because a child's talent can lead more quickly to having a fixed mindset and the inability to deal with loss or setbacks, especially if the talented child loses to someone with less talent than they do.

Parents and their young athletes have to combat a societal belief system that values talent and winning over everything else in the sports world.

Since Dr. Dweck's original publication on mindset, the idea has gone past just how we educate and also into how we work. Several large companies have adopted growth mindset strategies into training their managers. As a result, the culture many companies use to create productivity is shifting to a growth mindset-oriented management system.

This new way of thinking in the "real world" is essential for kids in their late teens to understand because it will help them enter the workforce, either after high school or after college.

At the end of this book, I will share many of the resources available to parents to increase their knowledge and teaching tools.

Embedding a culture, or Incorporating a culture.

Behavioural competencies

Embracing a culture of encouragement.

GROWTH MINDSET.

Moving forward

1

THE SCIENCE OF MINDSETS

THE IMPORTANCE OF MINDSETS

A person's mindset shapes the way they think, learn, and behave. Unfortunately, many children develop a fixed mindset from an early age. This fixed-minded set is what it sounds like. It is fixed so it doesn't change throughout a person's life. This is not the best way to learn and grow as a person.

According to the research done by a group called 7 Mindsets, less than 10% of adults ever reach the goals they set for themselves. This leaves over 90% of people who can't or doesn't reach the goals they have set (*How to Change Your Mindset*, 2016).

This statistic led the people of 7 Mindsets to understand the difference between the sub 10% of people who achieve their goals and the rest who do not achieve their goals.

They concluded that those who can achieve their goals have a different and more learning-oriented mindset. This mindset allows them to deal with failure and succeed in learning failures along the way.

This more positive and growth-oriented mindset appears to be what sets them apart. A fixed mindset usually causes a person to be more pessimistic about their abilities to succeed at the new things they try. It doesn't allow for the necessary changes and brain growth that need to occur to complete a new task correctly.

==With the right mindset, a child can and will grow into an intelligent and successful adult. Here is how to get them there.==

HOW THE BRAIN WORKS

There has been some research in the areas of mindset and brian malleability called neuroplasticity. Though there hasn't been a great deal of study of the mindsets by neurologists, what has been learned is quite significant.

Some neuroscientific research has shown that the brain is "malleable." Therefore, the brain itself and the brain's chemistry can be changed and improved.

The brain changes with new experiences by expanding neurons through growing hair-like tendrils called dendrites. These dendrites meet up with other dendrites from an adjacent neuron at points called synapses in an exceptional web of neurons. Synapses send messages back and forth to other parts of the brain. The more dendrites and synapses you have in your "neural pathway," the easier it is to learn and adapt.

The neural pathway is how the brain sends messages to the rest of the systems in the human body. The ability to send these messages helps us to solve problems more efficiently.

The growth of synapses takes off for humans at about seven years old. The brain creates a very dense web of neurons. So thick that the brain has to start trimming out the lesser-used neurons, so the thriving ones have room to expand. As humans learn new things and have unique experiences, many neurons grow more robust, causing weaker ones to die off and be trimmed out. By getting rid of the lesser or never used ones, the brain changes with the person as they grow and change by getting rid of the lesser or never used ones.

Having a growth mindset enables your mind to grow and change. People with a growth mindset are more willing to do new and different things leading to dendrite growth. People with a fixed mindset tend not to try new things or give up before their brain begins to expand the webs of neurons.

Studies have also shown that part of the growth mindset has internalized incentives to do new things, which leads to increased dopamine levels. Dopamine is a naturally occurring chemical in the brain that helps a person feel pleasure and happiness. It is produced when someone is experiencing something they like.

The research shows that a person's IQ is not set when they are born, which used to be the expected belief. The school of thought among psychologists and neuroscience researchers is that some people are born with high IQs, but most people were born with average IQs meaning that your genes determined your Intelligence.

New research starting in the 1980s shows that this simply isn't true. Instead, there is evidence that the brain can grow new dendrites, synapses, and neurons, increasing a person's Intelligence. This means that with the right mindset, a person can actively improve their level of Intelligence.

The research that has led us to the discovery of mindsets is mainly driven by data collected from studies of achievements, motivation, overall increases in Intelligence, and other measurable changes to a person's learning capacity. Unfortunately, there is not a lot of research involving neuroscientists testing the brain itself for changes.

HOW CAN MINDSETS BE CHANGED?

The above section talked about how the brain works and how your mindset can change your brain. So if a person can improve their Intelligence by learning, they can also change the way they think.

Changing your child's mindset from fixed to growth is not only possible but can be done early on in the child's learning life. It is vital to maintain the growth mindset once it is achieved. It is also possible to return to a fixed mindset if the growth mindset is not nurtured.

This leads to the question of what a parent can do to shift their child's mindset away from the fixed, stagnant mindset to the ever-growing and improving growth mindset.

In the 1990s, Dr. Carol Dweck and her colleagues in the psychology department at Stanford University began studying the effects mindsets had on school-aged students. It was Dr. Dweck who discovered and named mindsets as fixed or growth (*Growth Mindset Programs*, 2019). This later became a spectrum starting with fixed and leading to growth with mixed mindsets in between, but there is less research in that area.

Dr. Dweck went into lower-performing schools with many students at or below the poverty line and racial and socioeconomic biases. Many of these students knew they were expected to fail or only reach an average level of Intelligence. She then taught the students how to improve their mindset by showing them some neuroscience findings on brain plasticity or our ability to change and mold our brains to be better, faster, and wiser. Brain plasticity can not only be the way your brain is structured but the way it functions, leading to a more efficient brain.

An example in one article about Dr. Dweck's research experiment (*Teacher Practices*, 2012) showed that a group of 7th graders who were taught about the ability to improve their learning increased their average math GPA from about a 2.5 to a 2.8. In contrast, in the control group, who were not taught about growth mindset and brain plasticity, GPAs decreased as the math became more complicated.

Several other studies have shown positive growth for students who were taught about creating a growth mindset for themselves.

There is a case study of an entire school teaching their students about growth mindset, but the principal and the teachers also learned ways to foster a growth mindset naturally. The results were positive and promising for other schools in the future.

As a former teacher, I found this study to be fascinating. One of the most significant ways the teachers could change the students' mindsets was through praise. But the one caveat to using praise is that if you don't use it correctly, you will only solidify the students' fixed mindsets instead of changing them to a growth mindset.

Often in a classroom, you will hear a teacher tell a student how smart they are for succeeding at a task. I used the phrase myself many times before I learned about the growth mindset. Telling a student they are smart is harmful praise from a growth mindset standpoint. This is because you need to praise a student for working hard. If you tell them they are smart, you are not giving them the proper motivation to continue working hard and increasing their learning. They now believe they are already smart, so they don't need to change.

Dr. Dweck and the teachers she worked with discovered that the students who received praise for doing hard work and succeeding wanted to continue working hard to be even more successful. Their motivation was not to work to be better at things they already knew but to work hard to learn how to do new things.

This type of praise also sets them up to be more prepared for being unsuccessful at a task. Because their mindset is to work hard, they can find better solutions to problems or difficulties they come across. The students who were told they were brilliant didn't have the same motivation to solve the challenges.

As a parent, you can learn from this study also. Make sure you are praising your child for working hard and trying. Even if they are unsuccessful at the task, they are trying. This will teach them to attempt to do something; even if they fail, they grow those critical connections in their brains. It is the action of working that helps them get more competent, not getting the answer correct.

I will go into more detail and give examples for parents in Chapter 4.

The growth mindset can also help improve the capabilities of a child with a learning disability or developmental delay or even those with an intellectual disability. The growth mindset will not cure any learning conditions, but it can strengthen a child's ability to deal with the setbacks caused by a learning disability.

With the correct type of praise, a child with a learning disability can discover ways to get around some of their difficulties if they are taught that they will have setbacks. Still, if they work hard and grow and strengthen the synapses in their brains, they will be able to do much more than was initially possible.

The key to helping a child with a learning disability like dyslexia or ADD/ADHD is to help them find ways to overcome the issues they have with processing information. With a growth mindset, their brain will still misfire, but it will grow those all-important dendrites that will improve the parts of the brain that are not causing the processing issues. With a growth mindset, a child with a processing issue is more likely to find ways to compensate for their particular case and be more optimistic and successful.

Tips for Changing Mindsets

Many different factors influence a child's mindset in their lives. Here are seven steps to reset a child or young adult's mindset.

Evaluate their way of thinking

The first thing a person should realize when having difficulty in life is to rethink their thinking. Being successful at a class, a job, or even a relationship is facilitated by their way of thinking. If something is not working, their mindset may need a new evaluation. There is something to be said about having an excellent education or learning specific new skills, but sometimes knowledge is not enough to succeed.

In most 12-step programs, the first step is to admit that you have a problem with whatever it is trying to help you. The same reasoning applies to a person's mindset. You can have all the skills you can learn, but if you still have a fixed mindset about success and failure, you will not change your outcome at your class or job.

Find the negative thoughts.

The second thing you need to do is find the negative mindset. All humans have something our subconscious mind tells us is wrong with us or that we are doing incorrectly. These thoughts can be even more prominent in young children who are still learning what success means. For example, some children think that missing 2 + 2 means they are a total failure. They must know these thoughts are not correct.

Children and adults need to pay attention to their negative thoughts. Bring them up to the surface of the conscious mind.

Fight back

Once the negative thoughts have been identified, it is now possible to push them aside. Now that you and your child know that those pesky negative thoughts tell them they can't finish their homework because it is too hard, they will now understand that these thoughts are inaccurate. Help them discover that it is possible to complete the assignment as long as they ignore their minds' negativity.

Remember how you got there.

Have your child think about how they got to their mindset and what things caused them to feel the way they do. Parents and teachers can use the good praises, but children are usually influenced more by their peers, social media, and the ever-changing world around them. Find out what affects their thoughts and their mindset.

Help them understand that all their experiences shape who they are and how they think. A thorough evaluation of the way they interpret their surroundings will help you and your child get a better idea of how they got to their thought process up to this point.

Also, remember that young children don't think in the same way as most adults, so something that you are doing or saying that you feel is benign can influence them in a very different way.

Knowing how they came to think the way they do will help set the tone for changing that thought process for the better in the future.

Understand that it takes more than motivation and willpower

Motivation and willpower are great tools to have, but our willpower will only go so far with all humans. Children have even less willpower than adults. Parents and children need to understand that not having enough willpower to start or complete a difficult task is normal. We often inadvertently or sometimes even on purpose make another person feel bad or guilty for giving in to distraction. If a child feels guilty for giving in to a "want" or giving up their willpower, it could lead them away from the growth mindset they are trying to achieve.

Instead of feeling guilty, you and your child should accept that sometimes humans do not follow the plan they put in place. Willpower is not an easy thing to adhere to. Your child will make decisions that go against their willpower. Tell them this is part of life. They are still learning what willpower is.

A child's motivation will sometimes wane, just like willpower. Again being unmotivated is a common human trait.

Sometimes these two things just run out. But with a positive growth mindset losing motivation and willpower will not last long. The growth mindset will help them reestablish control.

Take one step first.

The more complex the task is, the harder it is to have the correct mindset going in. Children can sometimes take on massive goals. "I want to make straight A's on my report card" is a great goal, but what happens when they get a B? They now can't accomplish their goal. They are forced to give up. This makes them feel like a failure because they didn't achieve their goal.

When building a positive or growth mindset, a child needs to have success at something. So completing a small task successfully or accomplishing a small goal will succeed at more complex, more complicated functions down the road.

Instead of wanting to make straight A's for the entire grading period, tell them to set a goal to improve the number of questions they answer correctly on their next test. This is a much easier and quicker goal to accomplish. The sooner they start to see results, the better.

In many cases, children in upper grades have to solve multi-step math problems. Some children look at this complicated math problem and see an overwhelming task. But if the first step is a simple addition, ask them to complete only the first step. This will give them the success they need and feel less overwhelmed.

> Do just the first step. Succeed. Take a break. Then come back and do step one and step two. Build on the success of the first step.

Know that failure is OK

This tip is the most important thing to understand if you want to get your child to a growth mindset.

Failure is OK. It is more than OK. Failure is an essential part of growth. But, unfortunately, many children feel that if they make a mistake or get a question wrong, they are letting themselves and everyone around them down. This is simply the wrong way to think.

When I was teaching, and my students would get upset about getting things wrong, I would always point out famous people who got something wrong. My favorite is the story of Thomas Edison failing at creating the incandescent light bulb over a thousand times before he brought it to work. I used his example because most elementary school curriculum teaches children about inventors, including Thomas Edison.

Pointing out that Thomas Edison and other inventors failed at something helps a child let go of the "If I get something wrong, I am a failure" thought process. Thomas Edison failed repeatedly, but he learned from each try that the combination of materials he was using did not work to make the light bulb illuminate. Those failures are what led him to success. He put in the effort until he finally found the right combination of materials.

Teach your child that failure is as much a part of life as success is. Without failure, there would be no invention or innovation. They will fail. No one is perfect, so everyone fails at something. Their mindset will determine how they deal with these inevitable failures.

We now know that the brain can be changed and improved by learning. Children learn best by getting something wrong and then figuring out how to get to the correct answer. Failure is a part of success. Understanding that failure is good is essential to gaining and maintaining a growth mindset.

COMMON MISCONCEPTIONS ABOUT THE GROWTH MINDSET

Dr. Dweck has spent some time since her book was published in 2006. She was correcting some of the assumptions made by readers about growth mindsets.

One of the things she talks about is false growth mindsets, in which you think you have a growth mindset or misunderstood what a growth mindset is. She has also made it clear that a growth mindset is not permanent once you have it, nor does it pertain to all aspects of your life.

A person can have a growth mindset but then face a triggering moment that catapults the person back to a fixed mindset. This can happen when a person has a very proud skill but then meets someone much better at that skill. It can cause feelings of inadequacy that make the person think they aren't that good after all.

I have seen this happen a lot in the world of writing. I have written things that I thought were good, only to read something on the same topic that is much better written. I had to convince myself that I would get better if I practiced my writing and learned from better writers to keep my growth mindset. This was not easy for me or for some colleagues who also lost confidence in their writing skills. It is much easier to give up than put in the work to improve your mindset and abilities.

Another misunderstanding of the growth mindset is praise. I talked about effective ways to praise children earlier in this chapter. When inflating the process, not the outcome, you must clarify that you honor the process that leads to improved development.

Parents and teachers should not praise a child who worked hard but used the wrong strategies and had a bad outcome. Raising a child just for working hard is not enough. It could reinforce incorrect strategy, which will not improve grades or lead to high order thinking skills. This misuse of praise can also show a struggling child to have a more entrenched fixed mindset. When a child receives recognition for working hard but doesn't improve, they start to think they can't improve. For example, a teacher praises a child for working hard on a math problem with regrouping, but the problem is entirely wrong. They are hearing the teacher say, "Well, at least you tried, but you just don't get it."

Dr. Dweck has begun to emphasize the use of correct learning strategies that lead to growth and improvement. Instead of praising the child working on regrouping for trying, praise them for wanting to learn, then show them a different way to do the problem that might lead to a better outcome.

The goal of praise is to reward a person for doing things correctly and for improving self-esteem. If a parent or teacher praises a child for just trying, but there is still a negative outcome, then that child's self-esteem will still take a hit. Children are aware of how well or poorly they are progressing. Therefore, it is crucial to give them the best strategies for success and the right kind of praise.

Academic coach and tutor Chris Loper remind people that a growth mindset is a process and will not happen overnight, nor is it a miracle cure to learning struggles (Loper, 2021).

Having a growth mindset is essential to increasing a child's learning ability, but other strategies and techniques need to be used in conjunction with a growth mindset. This is especially true for children and adults with processing disorders, dyslexia, or ADHD. In addition, a growth mindset can not be the only strategy for children in low-income environments or whose parents struggle with a lack of education.

Loper writes in his blog that teaching children about growth mindset and telling them they should have one is not going to cut it when getting a person to shift from a fixed mindset to a growth mindset. They need to see a growth mindset in action.

In other words, when a child comes across a concept they are struggling with, walk them through a strategy to solve the idea to show them that the right approach will help them grow and learn.

Another problem that may arise with creating a growth mindset is how most school systems are designed. Many of them have an emphasis on using standardized tests in school to determine a student's growth. Even if you have a growth mindset, you can still do poorly on standardized tests. In many of the tests, I have administered a good portion of the test. A timed test can use a different strategy to solve a problem if the first one used did not work. In these cases, a child with a growth mindset may still appear not to be successful.

The school system also honors and rewards brilliant children by giving them great accolades for doing well on standardized tests. They get rewards, medals, and sometimes even scholarships to high schoolers who make perfect scores on their SAT or ACT. These actions promote a fixed mindset for both the child being rewarded and those around them.

This also happens with students who are put in AP classes and gifted programs. They are being told by the school system that they are unique because they are more intelligent than other students. So these schools are modeling fixed mindset beliefs. Most schools assign letter grades on report cards without using the percentages that correspond with that letter. There is significant growth from a 30% F to a 65%F, but all the child and parents see is an F, not the 35% growth. The school still considers an F a failure, but sure, students' failure rates might change if the child was graded on their growth percentage. Celebrate growth even if your child has an F and makes a higher percentage F on the next report card.

As a parent, it is hard to control what happens at school or among your child's peers, but if you keep working, you can promote the growth mindset and hope your child can overcome the other fixed mindset triggers around them.

Chris Loper's blog post also mentions that a growth mindset will not happen overnight. It takes a long time and a lot of work to change from a fixed mindset to a growth mindset. He also points out that everyone has some fixed and some growth mindsets, and that is normal. Most people will never have a complete growth mindset about every aspect of their lives.

The strategies given in this book are effective, but many will need to become lifelong practices. There are no shortcuts to a growth mindset. If a person takes a shortcut, they create a false growth mindset, which can be worse than a fixed mindset.

2

GROWTH MINDSET AND EMOTIONAL INTELLIGENCE

In the last chapter, I explained the difference between a fixed mindset and a growth mindset. In this chapter, I will explain the correlation between emotional intelligence and the growth mindset.

Understanding emotional intelligence is crucial to understanding and creating a growth mindset. Moving from a fixed mindset to a growth mindset will be impossible without a firm grip on our emotions.

WHAT IS EMOTIONAL INTELLIGENCE?

Emotional Intelligence sometimes referred to as emotional quotient (EQ), is a person's ability to process, understand, and interpret the nuances of their own emotions and the emotions of the people around them. (*Growth Mindset and Emotional Intelligence*, 2020).

According to the website Verywell Mind, there are four levels of emotional Intelligence you as a parent should be aware of as you and your child journey through life and ever-changing emotional stimuli. (https://www.facebook.com/verywell, 2019).

Levels of Emotion

The emotion levels here are in order from basic to more complex. Most people, even children, can master the lower levels quite quickly. But the last level is where children and adults alike struggle. It is also where the growth mindset and growing cognitive thinking comes into play.

Level 1: Intuiting emotions

This means a person understands emotions at a fundamental level. The person can decipher facial expressions and body language. They can tell if the people around them are happy, sad, or mad, but they may not understand why they have this emotion.

This kind of emotional intuition is usually learned at a very young age. It is understood just by being around other people. For example, small children associate a smile with happiness and a frown with sadness. At this level, there is not much reasoning as to why this person has these particular emotions.

The child knows what the emotions are, but that is where the information stops.

Level 2: Thinking through emotions

Thinking through emotions is when a person uses reasoning and cognitive skills to prioritize their attention. They determine whether or not a person across the room's feelings are more important than the emotions of the people closest to them.

In this stage of emotional intelligence, the child may discern a need to leave an angry person alone but decide it is OK to associate with the smiling person.

They are also learning more about their own emotions. They may not want to play with a person who was mean at recess. They won't understand why the other child was mean. They know that they are saddened by someone being mean and won't play with that person next time. They may use their intuitive EQ to pick the smiling child next time they are at recess.

Level 3: Realizing meaning in emotions

Emotions are complicated. This level goes beyond identifying happy, sad, or angry from a chart of faces with different expressions or selecting the smiling kid on the playground.

It is one thing to know that someone is mad. It is another thing for a child to understand why another person could be angry and whether or not that anger is directed toward them.

There are a lot of reasons a person can be angry. They may have gotten a phone call with bad news or been in a fight with their significant other. They could very well be mad at the child observing them. Being able to understand the different reasons for specific emotions is vital in cognitive growth.

At this level, the child can now understand why they feel the way they do. They begin to make connections between actions and emotions. For example, they know that someone was mean to them, and that action made them sad or angry. This can lead to the ability to decide that they don't want to be mean because if it makes them sad, it will more than likely make someone else miserable.

The child can now synthesize information about emotions and make behavioral decisions based on this information. This process is a little easier for children leaning toward a growth mindset. The child now understands that their actions can change the outcome of an emotion-provoking encounter. A child with a fixed mindset may be less inclined to change their behavior because they are not expecting the result of the meeting to change or be influenced by their action.

Level 4: Mastering emotions

Mastering emotions is pretty self-explanatory in its definition, but it is rather complex in its execution in reality.

This is the level where a person can understand the nuances of human emotions and regulate their own emotions. The child can interpret the feelings around them and adjust their behavior or responses to the corresponding emotion in the correct socially appropriate way.

It is challenging to navigate emotional situations correctly all the time. Even after reaching this level, there will be times that a child, or even a well-adjusted adult, will misinterpret a situation. This does not mean that the child has lost some of their emotional Intelligence. It just means the child is human. A growth mindset will allow the child to move past the awkward misinterpretation and prepare for the subsequent passionate encounter.

Measuring Emotional Intelligence

Some researchers believe that a person's emotional intelligence plays a more critical role in their success than their IQ.

A couple of tests that a parent and an emotional health specialist may use to measure their own or a child's EQ.

The Mayer-Salovey-Caruso Emotional Intelligence Test (MSCEIT) (Cherry, 2020) is one that the subject fills out independently. It helps to measure the four levels of emotional Intelligence. The levels may have slightly different names, but they are the same basic concepts mentioned above. It uses scaled questioning about the way the subject feels or perceives emotions as the metric for determining the level of emotional Intelligence,

The Emotional and Social Competency Inventory (ESCI) (Cherry, 2020) is based on older concepts of emotional intelligence research. This test is filled out by the people around the subject being tested. It uses observational data based on others' interpretations of the subject's behaviors and emotions as the metric to determine the subject's emotional Intelligence.

There are other tests scattered around the internet, but these two are widely recognized as being based on research with a high level of accuracy.

EMOTIONAL INTELLIGENCE AND A FIXED MINDSET

A child with a fixed mindset can experience emotional deviation at the first sign of failure. In her book "Mindsets," Dr. Dweck gives many different examples of what this looks like.

Failure equates to being a loser, stupid, or several other derogatory and harmful terms that a child could believe about themselves. If they fail at it, they feel that they can't do the task at hand and should give up.

The child with a fixed mindset believes that they have a set of abilities and they are as intelligent as they will ever be. They think that they can not expand their capabilities past what they were born with.

That is why when they fail at something, they make little effort to learn from the failure or make an effort to correct the things they got wrong.

Children and adults with a fixed mindset are embarrassed by their failures. They believe that everything they do is a measure of who they are and how smart they are. One loss can derail an entire life of growth and potential.

A brainwave study at Columbia yielded some validating information on the idea of mindsets (Dweck, 2006).

When they studied a person's brain with a fixed mindset, they could only see interest in things they got right when asked hard questions. These subjects showed no sign of interest in wrong answers. They also showed no discernible attention to answers to those questions that were wrong. They had no interest in learning from their mistakes.

The subjects with a growth mindset wanted to learn from their mistakes, so they showed interest in what they missed and how to correct them.

Dr. Dweck also talks about depression in college students in her book. The students with a fixed mindset tend to give up altogether. Many stop going to class and stop turning in their work. This, of course, leads to more failure, which can lead to more depression.

Students with a growth mindset tended to have more coping skills and could fight the depression enough to continue going to classes and completing their assignments.

There has been a sad trend in the last few years of much younger children suffering from depression and thoughts of being inadequate. It was reported that some of these younger kids believe they are depressed because they are not good enough at something. Their emotional intelligence is not fully developed. If they also had a fixed mindset, it would be complicated to overcome a catastrophic failure.

Children with a fixed mindset are also prone to cheating to keep looking smart. They are so emotionally devastated at "being a failure" that they will do anything to hide it from those around them. They see no point in studying because that is a futile effort. But, they cannot let themselves be seen as a failure.

This need to cheat can be carried up to adulthood and into a career. There have been journalists who have made up stories and sources just to get ahead of the game. These same people, with some effort, could have probably gotten ahead anyway. CEOs refused to change their product because they did not want to admit that their ideas were inadequate or obsolete. A fixed mindset can cause a lot of emotional damage to the people involved in these nefarious activities.

A fixed mindset can impede the development of a child's emotional Intelligence. Without reaching the highest levels of EQ, life can be challenging to navigate well.

EMOTIONAL INTELLIGENCE AND GROWTH MINDSET

Emotional intelligence and growth mindsets are intricately connected. We have already discussed the concept of neuroplasticity. Both emotional intelligence and growth mindsets trigger growth in the human brain. When a child learns how to get to the higher levels of emotional intelligence, they are growing and improving the dendrites and synapses in their brains just like they do when they are open to a growth mindset.

A child with a growth mindset can get to the highest level of emotional Intelligence more rapidly than a child with more nominal growth within the brain due to a fixed mindset. Higher levels of emotional Intelligence reciprocally help the child to maintain the positive attitude and synapsis growth associated with the growth mindset.

The growth mindset leads to healthier emotional choices. These healthier choices lead to better coping skills and an all-around better vibrant life.

6 WAYS TO TEACH YOUR CHILD GOOD EMOTIONAL INTELLIGENCE

Step one: Name their emotions.

With children, it is a good idea to talk about their emotions. For example, talk about what anger is and what it means. Give the feeling of frustration a name and a definition. Feelings are abstract. Children have more difficulty understanding things that they cannot touch or see. By giving emotions names, it makes them more tangible. A child knows what to call a particular emotion. The name brings the emotion that is somewhere in the cosmos into view right in front of them.

Once your child understands how to articulate their emotions, they will start learning how to deal with their feelings more positively and healthily.

Make sure you also name the positive emotions and not just the negative ones. Sometimes we as parents or educators rush to get a child to understand how to deal with emotions that lead to undesired behaviors. Positive emotions can be just as powerful as negative ones. A child needs to know and understand how to react to the excitement, pride, and happiness. These emotions do not generally lead to inappropriate behavior, so we talk about positive emotions less often.

Step two: Show Compassion

In many cases, when an upset child begins crying or acting out negatively, the adult wants to ignore the behavior or fuss at the child for being upset. Unfortunately, this tendency is not the best way to react. If you tell the child to stop, fuss at them, or pretend they are not acting out, you reinforce the thought that they are doing something wrong.

There is nothing wrong, harmful, or disrespectful about experiencing powerful emotions. For example, if you fuss at the child for crying, you ignore whatever made them share a sad feeling.

You must show compassion and understanding for what your child is going through. They may be mad because they dropped their snack on the floor, and now they don't have their snack. It is upsetting because their mistake made them unable to have something they wanted.

Tell them that you understand what they are experiencing. Explain that you get upset when you drop food or other things too.

Responding empathetically shows them that it is OK to have feelings and that their feelings are valid. Once they know you understand them and that having feelings and emotions is a normal part of life, it will help them react more positively to their simple mistakes. For example, now that they know the adults around them have the same feelings, it will be easier to ask for a new snack instead of crying or sulking.

Step three: Show off the correct way to deal with emotions.

Most children learn by watching the people and world around them. So parents' or caregivers' actions have the most significant influence on how they learn the appropriate ways to react to emotions.

Parents should talk openly about emotions and the subsequent reaction to those emotions. Discuss your responses to emotions with your child and explain why you reacted the way you did. For example, if you lost your temper and misbehaved, admit that you did not respond in a socially acceptable manner. Pointing out samples of the wrong emotional response can be just as teachable a moment as exhibiting the correct reaction.

The way you express your emotions will, in turn, be the way your child learns to express their feelings. For example, suppose you lose your temper but don't explain that your reaction was adverse. In that case, your child will internalize the incorrect response, thus making them think that losing one's temper is a socially acceptable emotional reaction.

You, as a parent, must have good emotional intelligence and a positive mindset before you teach it to your children.

Step four: Demonstrate positive ways to cope

Once a child has learned their emotions, and why they are happening, it is time to deal with them. Unfortunately, most children have a difficult time learning to process negative emotions. Even if they have watched their parents and teachers, and other adults navigate smoothly through negative emotions, it is still hard for a child to regulate their feelings as the feelings are happening to them. For example, many adults stop thinking clearly when they are mad. Likewise, we can't expect a child to think clearly during an emotional outburst.

Children need immediate and appropriate feedback about their reactions to learning. If you wait too long, the child will have moved on from that emotion, and the input won't be processed. Using visual prompts and reminders of dealing with confusion, anger, and frustration can trigger a memory of the correct reaction.

After an emotional outburst, children try to understand what they did wrong. This would be an excellent time to role-play the events that caused the emotional explosion. If role-playing makes the child uncomfortable, use a fictitious scenario similar to the actual events. Make sure the child plays other roles besides the one they experienced. Seeing other people's perceptions of them can sometimes give the child more insight into their emotional reaction.

These strategies work just as well with younger children, prepubescent children, and preteens.

Strategies to create emotional awareness using the growth mindset in teens and young adults will be discussed in Chapter 6.

With younger children, creating an emotions box can help the child process emotions. The box is meant to keep their strategies and activities to aid in automated their emotions all-in-one in a convenient place.

In this box, your child can put in coloring pages, Play-Doh, or other activities that are calming. If they need visual prompts, go through old magazines and create emotion cards with a picture on one side and an explanation on the other. If visuals are not required, the child or their parents can write down reminders of strategies like "Take a deep breath and count to ten," "Breathe in through your nose and out of your mouth," or "Think about someplace you would want to visit."

Once your child has the tools to reinforce what they have learned about coping with emotions, let them decorate the box (or another kind of container they choose). This will give them positive emotions by having ownership of this box. The more memorable it is to them, the more likely they will use it when they need it. The more likely the things inside will help them cope and help them associate positive emotions while improving their emotional Intelligence and creating a growth mindset going forward.

Different strategies work for different children. Some kids might find a yoga pose relaxing, while others might find a funny YouTube clip as a way to calm down. There have been many studies about the calming effects of certain types of music.

Sometimes parents or teachers have to dig deep into their coping skills and emotional Intelligence to gracefully ignore the music that a child uses to recenter themself.

I would be OK with never hearing "Let it Go" from the movie Frozen ever again, but it helps calm and the center one of the young men I work with who has an intellectual disability. So I smile and sing along so that he can cope with his emotions. You, as a parent, have to be able to grit your teeth and deal with it if that one annoying song helps your child.

By allowing your child outlets to process their emotions, you create a more positive and growth-oriented state of being.

Don't also forget to help them cope with positive emotions too. Sometimes excitement can overwhelm a child just as much or more than anger or fear. Some children can get physically ill if they get over-excited.

The same calming techniques can be used for excitement. However, it may take longer to deal with excitement because it can be linked to an event or activity that hasn't happened yet.

Anger is linked to an emotional response to something that has already happened. Once the child has processed the anger, they can move on. But with excitement or anticipation, the event causing the emotion has not happened yet. The overexcitement can then be a recurring emotion until the event that led to the excitement has occurred.

Step five: Hone their skills at problem-solving

Coping skills are essential to master when a child is approaching the highest level of emotional intelligence, but there is also a need to problem-solve. Sometimes problems will come up, and the solution is not in the emotions box.

This is where the emotional intelligence and growth mindset intersect. One of the critical components of the growth mindset is learning new things from your successes and failures. This is also a key component of Emotional Intelligence.

If a difficulty arises, a growth mindset helps to give the child the confidence to find a workable solution to the problem. So this leads to the ability to problem-solve when new, different, or overwhelming emotions emerge that the child may not completely understand.

When new and different emotions show up, a child will be overwhelmed by their emotion, or they will use their growth mindset and emotional intelligence to formulate a way to cope without being overwhelmed.

A child who can solve problems regarding their emotions will translate that same skill into solving more fundamental issues.

Step six: Never stop teaching emotional Intelligence

Emotional Intelligence is not something that you memorize and never have to think about again. It is an ongoing process that never eliminates, especially as the child gets older. The world and emotions get more complicated as a child grows into a teen and then an adult.

At some point, the child will outgrow the emotion box. It will no longer be relevant to the new emotions of puberty or the feelings caused by more complicated and rigorous academics. However, your child may be able to update the emotions box if that works for them.

Things like making and losing friends, getting bad grades because the subjects get more challenging, or even simple things like their favorite show getting canceled can upset the balance they established when they were younger.

With more complicated emotions comes a need for much more complex strategies for regulating emotions. You, as a parent, must continue talking about feelings as often as possible. You can use real-world examples or fictional characters to start a meaningful and productive discussion about what happened in the news, a book, or a show. The debate will only be compelling if the examples are something your child can relate to. Let them decide where the discussion should start.

Ask questions about what happened in the news or a story? What were the emotional responses of the involved parties? Were the responses socially appropriate for the situation? Ask your child what they would have done in that scenario. Discuss if their solution would be better or worse. Tell them what you would have done in the scenario as well. Get feedback on how your solution and their solution are similar and different. Never tell them they are wrong about their response. Instead, offer them logical alternative solutions. They may have some alternatives for you to think about as well.

Never stop the dialogue. The more you discuss emotional Intelligence, the more thinking they will do and the more dendrites they will grow.

3

COVID-19 AND THE GROWTH MINDSET

Without a doubt, the last year and a half have affected the entire world emotionally. So many people are coping with loss, anger, confusion, frustration, and many other challenging emotions.

Even people with great emotional intelligence and a positive attitude with the best growth mindset were affected.

CAN A GROWTH MINDSET HELP STUDENTS DURING THE PANDEMIC?

Four members of the faculty of Education at Henan Normal University in Xinxiang, China, studied how the growth mindset helped students at their university during the pandemic (Zhao et al., 2021). Xinxiang is in

Henan Province, which borders Wuhan Province. Henan Province was struck with COVID-19 outbreaks because of its proximity to Wuhan Province, where the pandemic began.

Due to the constraints of China's implementation of restrictive movement policies, the study was conducted online in a survey format. The survey was distributed to the teachers, who then disseminated it to their students online.

The student did not mention the effects that COVID-19 had on students with a fixed mindset. Instead, it concentrated on students that, based on the survey, had a growth mindset.

The bulk of these students looked at the perceived COVID-19 event strength and perceived stress (Zhao et al.) the student had because of the event strength. Perceived stress is the negative feelings like worry or tension due to a high-stress event. Perceived event strength is how far-reaching and influential the high-stress event is. In this case, the pandemic's perceived event strength was very high.

This study concluded that even though the event strength was very high along with the perceived stress, these students with a growth mindset could cope well with the pressures from the pandemic. They showed lower levels of perceived stress and had a higher engagement in their studies.

TIPS FOR HELPING YOUR CHILD MAINTAIN A GROWTH MINDSET IN THE TIME OF COVID-19.

These first tips have been given to teachers, but they will be suitable for parents as well. Especially if you are homeschooling or if your child is struggling with online learning.

Tip 1- Make a future goals poster

A great way to keep your child focused during the pandemic is to ask them to do a future goals poster. Future goals will help them realize that they are in a temporary situation that will pass. Their future plans can be day-to-day, as the need to finish class assignments, or long-term goals like learning to drive or getting a summer job.

The website Lexia suggests a visual poster that uses pictures from magazines or a child's drawing. That is a great option, but some children may want to write out words or even sentences. Let your child make the board however they feel will help them the most.

Tip 2- Write down their progress

Write down daily or weekly the progress you and your child have made towards those goals. This is most commonly done in the form of journaling. But, in this case, it should not be kept private. These writings are meant to be shared. You can even use them as conversation starters to discuss what is happening around them.

Tip 3- Create a "my growth" timeline

For children who like visual references, make a timeline showing their growth during these challenging times. They can see where they started and where they are now. Make sure to praise them for the progress they have made and all the hard work they have done so far.

I would recommend that you as a parent also do these activities with your child. Make your goal poster, keep your notebook on progress, and create a timeline that shows your growth and progress.

This pandemic has affected parents, so sharing these activities with your children can be just as therapeutic for you as a parent.

Motivation is an essential part of the growth mindset. Unfortunately, in many cases, when stressful events happen, it is hard to continue to put in the hard work to keep growing. The loss of motivation can set your child back towards a fixed mindset. The tips above are meant to combat this motivation loss, but you can do a few more things to keep up that internal motivation necessary for growth.

These additional tips are essential if you are homeschooling your child. If you are not, you can put these tips in play when asking your child to do chores around the house. Unfortunately, this pandemic has created a unique problem. Children have heard the phrase "Due to circumstances beyond our control…" way too many times in the past eighteen months.

Tip 1- Give them choices

If you are homeschooling, give them the choice of school-related activities. For example, for reading, provide them with an option to pick one out of two or three things on a list. Then give them an opportunity of how they want to explain the literary concepts of the story. Finally, provide them with the option of a standard book report, maybe a graphic novel format, or short story format.

If you ask them to do chores around the house, give a list of 3 or four different duties and ask them to pick two.

It is crucial when so many things are decided for them about what they have to do that they control some of the things they need to do. Of course, they still have to put in the work, but it helps them stay motivated if they decide on their own.

Tip 2- Help them with self-evaluation

Self-evaluation is essential to maintain motivation. When they have completed a portion of their school work, ask them how much time and effort they put into the assignment. Talk with them about what they learned from their hard work. Keep them thinking in terms of growth and hard work. Children know if they have put in enough effort. Sometimes having them say they did not put in the effort they should have will motivate them to do better next time. The children who put in the effort and see the fruits of their labor will want to continue their efforts.

Tip 3- Keep them connected

The worst part of this pandemic is the isolation it has caused in most of the world. Encourage your child (and yourself) to find ways to stay connected to other people outside of their immediate family. For example, many people learned to work by using platforms like Zoom or Microsoft Teams. This is an excellent way to play also, children can connect with friends online; there are even ways to watch movies together.

There have been many studies over the years done on the necessity for humans to connect. They have all come to the same conclusion; humans are social beings and need to communicate with other people to have good emotional intelligence.

It doesn't matter how your child connects with friends. Just make sure they can. If you usually take away a communication device as punishment for bad behavior, either find a different form of punishment or lessen the amount of time you keep them disconnected.

Covid has changed the way people function in the world. Those people with growth mindsets have fared better with the changes than those with fixed mindsets.

COVID-19 AND DISTANCE LEARNING

Many schools and businesses were forced to shut down because of COVID-19's rapid spread worldwide in early 2020. These massive shutdowns changed the way people live their everyday lives. This includes how we communicate, work, learn, and all the essential things humans must do to live.

Out of necessity, many communities around the world began experimenting with distance learning. It has long been the norm that children get up and leave their home to go to a particular building where they are schooled. It seems that there was a belief that this congregation of children was somehow the best and, to many, the only way to learn successfully.

The pandemic has challenged this belief in a big way. Children could no longer leave their homes to congregate with other children because it wasn't safe. So parents and educators needed to figure out how to continue educating children during this time.

There is no real precedent for what education in the age of COVID-19 should look like. During the 1918 Spanish Flu Pandemic, most of the world's children simply stayed home. They read if they had books, but there were very few options then, and no real education took place.

Now, we have the internet and a whole planet connected through technology, something that the children in 1918 couldn't even imagine. This connectivity has made it possible to change the way we can educate children.

We must do everything in the framework of social distancing. This is how the concept of distance learning came about. It, like most other new ideas, came from necessity.

The first challenge educators and parents needed to consider in distance learning was the best way to communicate. Teachers required to deliver a lesson to the children, and the children needed to give feedback to the teachers. The most common form of our idea of communication is to be in the same space as the other person. Not only do you get pretty effective verbal communication being in the same room, but there is also body language at play. Most people read body language to get a more accurate picture of how a person is feeling. With COVID-19 and distance learning, such as classing held on Zoom or other online platforms, it's much more challenging to discern body language. In-person learning has changed as well with the use of face masks. Facial expressions are the most common form of body language. With a show covering half of a teacher's face, it will be difficult for some students to understand what is being said fully.

Communication through an online application can still be effective; sometimes, it is even more effective. Teachers need to give information to students, and students need to be able to internalize the information provided and respond to that information. How teachers disseminate the information to students doesn't have to be done in a classroom in person anymore.

Teachers can give this information on an interactive video online platform while students can respond in real-time. But teachers can also record their lessons, allowing a student to watch the class later or more than once, then send a response in whatever format the teacher and the student feel comfortable . Thus, there are many different ways to use technology to deliver a lesson.

For parents, helping their child or teenager learn independently at home can get a little overwhelming. This is where having a growth mindset comes in. Of course, there are challenges, but with the right attitude and strategies, distance or at-home learning will become much more manageable.

According to the experts at educircles.org, using strategies is the best way to get past obstacles that may be hindering your child's ability to learn properly. But, before we go over the plan, parents need to understand that things will go wrong. For example, maybe a login doesn't work, a video won't play on your specific device, there is only one computer, and you need it for work, maybe the internet is spotty, or many other things. On top of those issues, sometimes the lesson is just too hard. Many parents can find it challenging to figure out some lessons or assignments without a teacher's training.

A child or a parent with a fixed mindset may just give up, not realizing that strategies can help. Using a growth mindset and growth strategies will help a child get through the tricky part.

Here are three strategies for when things just don't go right while doing distance learning from home.

"It Didn't Work Even Though I Tried. Can I Quit?"

1- Break the lesson or assignment up

Make the challenging assignments smaller. Break it up into smaller pieces. Do one step at a time. Some tasks or lessons don't have to be done to do the more straightforward parts first. It is easy to get overwhelmed and give up. Smaller, more manageable tasks are much less overwhelming.

2- Go back to the beginning

In cases of cechnology useage we often find challenges with the technoogy not working first time. In such cases you just need ot restart your computer or device and go from there.

This idea can work with most assignments that are difficult too. Go back to the beginning and start over. Your child might have missed part of the instructions that may be key to solving the problem. With distance learning, they don't have the help of a teacher to point out what they missed possibly.

3-Use the word "yet."

A person with a growth mindset believes that they can learn as long as they put in the effort. But when a child or a parent is amid overwhelming frustration, the action may begin to feel futile. In this case, remind yourself or your child that you just don't know this "yet."

Adding "yet" to the issue brings you back to the growth mindset and a more positive thought process. Just because you can not do the task now doesn't mean you cannot ever do it.

"I Can't Concentrate. I Want to do Something Else"

Working or learning from home also comes with the challenge of staying on task and completing work promptly. School buildings are designed to minimize distractions, and this is not so at home.

There are no TVs with full cable access or video game hookups in a school building, nor are there cell phones to look at. There is a designated time to go outside and to eat. All of these things are not regulated at home. As a result, there is a lot of temptation just to do other things.

Using a growth mindset, it is easier to deal with these less than ideal distractions. A child or a parent with a fixed mindset may try to procrastinate finishing assignments or allow the distractions to continue. Many parents think, "Well, my child is having fun outside with their friends right now; I will give them a few more minutes. Unfortunately, those few minutes can turn into hours.

Parents and children with a growth mindset understand the need to finish the assignments. But even with a growth mindset, distractions can creep up.

Here are three strategies to combat distractions.

First, pick a specific time to do the work.

Pick a time to do the assigned tasks. This way, you are not tempted to give your child "a few more minutes." For example, if you set a time to begin at 9:00 a.m., you and your child know how much outside time they get or how long they have to eat breakfast. Therefore, they cannot keep from doing the work by eating breakfast slowly.

Once you set a start time, you should probably schedule break times and an end time. Having scheduled break times can also help the strategy of breaking up challenging assignments.

Also, things are less overwhelming to a child when they know what time things will start and end. This strategy helps give them a similar structure to that of a typical school day. So there is less of a change to their daily lives.

Do it every day.

Having a start time and an end time is a great start, but they must also be consistent in the schedule. For example, starting at 9 a.m. one day and 11 a.m. the next can be confusing. It also doesn't build a good routine.

A daily routine is crucial to getting things done and staying on task. Once it is a habit, it is easy to get up and do the work without being overwhelmed.

Turn off everything but the work.

This strategy is the most difficult for both parents and children. Turn off the devices, stay away from friends in person and on social media when you have scheduled for the work to be done.

It is essential to be social during times of lockdowns and stay-at-home orders. Being social is part of having good emotional intelligence. However, some children may try to use being sociable as an excuse to stall. There is time to be social outside of the set time perimeters of online learning.

4

PARENTS

This whole book is about teaching a growth mindset to your child, but you as a parent have to have a growth mindset.

Every preflight safety talk tells you that oxygen masks will be released from above if the cabin is depressurized. Then, they say how to put on the cover and make sure air is flowing correctly. The last thing they say is, "if you are travel with a child or someone who needs assistance, put your mask on first before assisting your child."

As a child on a plane years ago, I heard that speech and wondered why my mom or dad would put their mask on before they could help me. So, as a curious child, I asked my mom why the airlines made it a rule that she couldn't help me first.

She did not sugar coat her answer. She said, "Well if I am not getting enough oxygen, I may pass out before I can finish helping you. Then neither of us will have oxygen. So I must make sure I can breathe first so that I can help you."

This is true in most aspects of life. If a parent does not put on their hypothetical mask first, no one breathes.

PUT YOUR GROWTH MINDSET MASK ON FIRST

Through my research, I have found a lot of information about what to do or say as a parent. We will get to that information later in this chapter. But first, as a parent teaching a growth mindset, you must make sure that you have a growth mindset to introduce this concept to your child.

It is challenging to have a growth mindset all the time. In an interview with Peter DeWitt in his online show "A Seat at the Table," Dr. Dweck points out that a person's mindset can shift depending on the activity they are doing. Life is much more complicated as a parent. There is more to do and keep up with a much greater emotional load (DeWitt, 2019).

These factors make it harder to be in a growth mindset all the time. But, to teach a child to reach a growth mindset and subsequently maintain the growth mindset, a parent must find a way to have a growth mindset in certain aspects of their thinking, mainly the ones that pertain to their children.

In the same video, Dr. Dweck points out that a person can have a growth mindset in one aspect of life and a fixed one in another. For example, a person could have a fixed mindset to tie up a trash can liner but have a growth mindset on their ability to improve their cooking skills.

HOW TO REACT TO FAILURE

In many ways, the growth mindset starts with the parents. It is a well-known fact that children learn by watching and interacting with the world around them in their early years. Babies and small children tend everything their parents do in the world, including their reactions to successes and failures.

In "Mindsets," Dr. Dweck tells the story of doting parents who tell everyone how smart a 3-year-old they have, but when he doesn't get into the best preschool, their adoration stops. It appears to them that he is a failure at 3. The fixed mindset of these parents will undoubtedly affect their son negatively for years to come.

Parents react to their failures as well as to their children's failures. But sometimes, parents do not respond in the same way to their disappointment as they do to their child's failure. Parents often believe it is okay if they fail at something, but somehow allowing their child to fall as something is damaging or detrimental to the child's emotional intelligence.

This school of thought leads children away from a growth mindset. Instead, when your child experiences failure, praise them for trying, then offer to help them figure out how to succeed at the failed task or encourage them to find the solution independently.

If your child fails at a task and you do it for them because they are frustrated or sad, you are showing them that failure is unacceptable.

My stepdaughter found tying her shoes to be a challenging task. Instead of making her deal with the frustration and trying different ways to learn to tie her shoes, my partner's ex allowed her to give up. Now she is 11 years old and will not wear shoes with laces because she can not tie them. My stepdaughter now believes that learning to tie her shoes is just too tricky, and she can never know to do it.

Her parents did not want to see her struggle, so they gave up. I told my partner how frustrated I was when I was learning to tie my shoes, but I kept trying until I knew how. Unfortunately, I was unable to persuade my partner or my stepdaughter that being frustrated was okay. And now, a few years later, my stepdaughter's fixed mindset is fully entrenched in who she is. I believe her to be a brilliant and creative child, but she thinks she is an average child who will be an average adult with no chance at greatness even though she is a talented artist. Her mother can produce much better art. My stepdaughter believes her mother is better not because she is older and has had more practice but because she was born with more talent. I told her she just needed to practice to be as good as her mom, but she decided that practicing was too tricky.

Children need to experience frustration and failure as part of life. Parents need to let them have these experiences. Experience is how a person grows their brain.

I have seen this same situation with other friends of mine. They don't want their children to struggle, so they keep a fixed mindset. But, unfortunately, there is a rising number of young adults who do not know how to deal with failure.

A former professor told us about her nieces and nephews who lived in New Jersey during Superstorm

Sandy. These children, like my stepdaughter, lived in a fixed mindset world along with their parents. They took the advice from my professor, who is from the Gulf Coast, and used to storms, and bought canned goods and non-perishable foods. The problem happened when it came to canned goods. There was no electricity, so their electric can opener did not work. The way my professor told it, they called her in a panic because they didn't know how to use a manual can opener. Because they all had been living with fixed mindsets, they didn't want the challenge of figuring it out. She had to explain step-by-step how to open the cans. A growth mindset would have created an environment where they could have figured out how to use the manual can opener more quickly so they could have eaten the food sooner.

PRAISE AND DISCIPLINE

I briefly talked about the importance of correct praising methods in chapter 1. Here I will give some examples of things parents say that sound like they should be the right thing to do but aren't.

Most parents love to see A's and B's on their child's report cards. More often than not, this is where the words "I am so proud of you; you are so smart" come out of the parent's mouth. The problem is that they are now sending their child into a fixed mindset. They now think that they are smart, so they don't need much effort.

What you should say is something like, "I am so proud of you! You worked so hard to make these grades. Keep up the good work." By praising their work to get to those A's and B's, you are sending them to the growth mindset. They now know that hard work pays off, and they should continue to work hard and study.

Now, I am not saying to tell your child they are wise; by all means, do so, but do it with the emphasis that hard work made them this smart. They are smart, but through hard work and a growth mindset, they can get even more intelligent.

Using the correct praising methods leads to using the accurate discipline methods. Discipline is a broad spectrum of reactions to a wide range of children's actions. In this section, I will talk about discipline from the learning and schooling standpoint.

Most schools have started sending school work home on Fridays for parents to check their child's progress. So you open up your child's folder and find sloppy, unfinished work. This makes you angry.

Some parents will fly off the handle by saying things like: "What is wrong with you?" or "This is the work of a stupid child," or "You are grounded until your work habits improve. Now go to your room." However, I have also seen cases where the parent told the child to finish the school work independently because they can do it; they just wouldn't do it at school.

In most cases, the child did not finish the work for a reason. The reason is rarely that the child is "just lazy." Punishing them for not being successful at something enforces the fixed mindset that they are just not good at things and never will be.

Now the child is in trouble for not finishing their work. A parent with a fixed mindset believes that their child should be doing better. There is no thought about why the school work is sloppy and unfinished. There is no thought that the child might not understand the work and needs more help.

I have encountered struggling children but refused to ask for help on their homework because their parents would tell them they should know it if they did it in class today or that only stupid kids wouldn't understand something as easy as that.

In contrast, a parent with a growth mindset will say things like, "How come you didn't finish your work? Do you need some help with it" or "This is pretty sloppy. Did you learn anything by doing it this way?" or "I see you didn't finish some of this work. Let's look at it together and see if I can help you figure it out."

As you may have guessed, the children with parents with a fixed mindset about their children's ability tend to continue with the sloppy, unfinished work. As a result, their grades tend to drop. On the other hand, the children with parents in a growth mindset tend to begin to improve after this conversation.

Parents must understand that children, even with a growth mindset, will not excel at all things.

My mother was an educator with a growth mindset approach to teaching. She had a growth mindset with her students as well as with my brother and me.

We discovered earlier on in my schooling that I could not spell my spelling words. Now, thirty years later, I still rely on spell check and a good editor. It turns out I have dyslexia. However, we did not know that until I was in 5th grade.

Instead of disciplining me for getting Fs in spelling, my mother worked with me on learning strategies to break words down. As a result, I never got higher than a C- on my elementary grade level spelling tests; we saw D's and C's as success. Over the years, using a growth mindset, I learned ways to overcome my inability to spell words correctly. It also gave me the confidence to continue writing even with this barrier of having spelling issues.

My 4th-grade teacher had a fixed mindset. To her, my inability to spell meant I was stupid and needed remedial reading classes. She also would punish me for failing my tests by taking away my recess to make me rewrite all the spelling words I missed ten times each. She believed that memorizing the comments was the only way to learn them. She also punished me for leaving the classroom during our class spelling bee. Finally, my teacher said that since I insisted I wasn't stupid, I had to participate.

I was lucky my mother wouldn't let these punishments stand. Instead, she and her growth mindset fought for me (and my brother) to create a learning and growth-oriented environment. Unfortunately, she could not change my 4th-grade teacher's mind, but she made sure that I understood that my teacher had the wrong way of thinking.

As a parent, you may find that your child is being punished by someone else with a fixed mindset. Continually cultivate a growth mindset at home and keep that mindset when dealing with others. An event like being penalized for mistakes can send a child back into a fixed mindset. However, if the parent deals with the issue and reminds the child that learning is about hard work, the child should regain a positive mindset.

When I was a resource teacher a few years ago, I had a student, "Brandon," with a reading disability; he also struggled with math. By the time I got him in 5th grade, everyone believed that he was just plain lazy. Brandon never did any work, and he was disruptive. His 5th-grade general education teachers all had fixed mindsets about him. One of them told me she didn't think he had a disability; he was just pretending so he didn't have to do anything in class.

I pulled Brandon into my room and just talked with him. It was clear he had a fixed mindset about himself. However, when I spoke with his mother later that day, it was clear she had given up too. She had once had a growth mindset about her son and his abilities, but after failing twice, she believed the teachers with a fixed mindset.

Brandon was one of my favorite students; he was very quick-witted and funny. We had some interesting conversations about life and tv shows. I worked hard with him to make him see he could learn, just in a different way.

What made me the saddest about his situation was that his mother had given up. Her growth mindset succumbed to the fixed mindsets around her, and she ended up with a fixed mindset herself.

I tell this story to point out that you have the power to change mindsets about your child as a parent rather than agree with them. Keep your growth mindset intact to ensure your child (even if they have learning barriers) keeps their growth mindset. With Brandon, just attempting to solve a problem was a victory. I was careful to praise the work he did. By the end of the year, he was making D's instead of F's. He had learned that hard work had improved his grades.

He went on to middle school the following year. I hope that he and his mother kept their new growth mindsets as he progressed. I ran into Brandon a few days ago at a local park. He said he is still working hard in high school. He was also happy because his teachers were more understanding and more likable than his 5th-grade teachers I knew. I am proud of him for doing well and continuing his hard work. His growth mindset will help him succeed in the workforce when he graduates in a few years.

The Way We Praise Others

There are parents out there who are familiar with the growth mindset. They praise their children in all the right ways, like for their efforts to learn.

However, they can forget that their children are still watching and learning from them. Some parents get frustrated with a creditor or someone on the road. They yell things like "That person is so stupid" or "I just can't deal with idiots today," or other similar terms. It can go the other way too. Say a parent is watching Jeopardy and says something about the winner like "That person is so smart" or "The guy is brilliant." The terms are used with a fixed mindset.

Now, your child could be confused about your mindset about them. Especially if they got a poor grade on a test, and you don't want to deal with idiots. Try to keep a positive growth mindset in all the things you say. Instead of calling a person stupid because you are frustrated with them, say something like, "I wish that person had more information for me about this situation." For the winner of Jeopardy, you could say something like, "I bet they worked very hard to learn those answers."

THE JUDGMENT OF CHILDREN

Many parents say they just "want what is best for their child," but in doing this, parents put expectations on their child. These are usually parents with a fixed mindset. They believe their child acts a certain way and likes certain things (usually something the parent likes).

If these expectations are not met, then the parents deem the child unworthy.

Sometimes these expectations go so far that the parent attaches their ability to love the child whether these expectations are met. This is a fixed mindset to the extreme. They feel their child is unworthy of their love because the fixed mindset tells them that if their child cannot do the things they think are great, then the child will not amount to anything.

Not all judgment goes to this extreme, but, in many cases, parents become disappointed in their child because the child was unable to do something that the parent equated to being successful.

I have often come across this attitude in my career as a teacher and a tutor for children.

This is the case with a student I recently began tutoring. The child "Elvis" is going into 2nd grade. He is struggling to read on his grade level, and he is distracted very easily. His father said to me in front of Elvis, "I don't know what to do with him. I don't have much hope that you can help him." There was a clear indication that he was very disappointed with his son.

As I worked with Elvis, I discovered a few things. One thing is Elvis' mother is from a Latin American country and speaks fluent Spanish. Elvis is fluent in Spanish as well. Now and then, he will let a Spanish word slip with his English. He struggles to read his sight words because they are much harder to sound out than words like cat or dog. Another thing I discovered is that this kid is funny and intelligent. With reminders to focus, he has learned most of his sight words in a concise time.

His father was disappointed because his son could not read well in English. In his fixed mindset, that was the most important thing. He failed to see that his son is bilingual and can go back and forth between the two languages pretty well for a 7-year-old. Elvis is easily distractible because of his vivid imagination. There is so much there to be proud of.

The whole two hours of our first tutoring session took me to convince Elvis he could learn these words with a little hard work. He believed he couldn't understand them because he, too, had a fixed mindset. Then, after only a few weeks, he surprised himself with his ability to read the words I had given him.

Elvis knew his father was disappointed in him and was glad to prove that he could learn these words and indeed did learn the words.

Another thing a parent needs to understand about failure and judgment is that siblings are not always good at the same things. Comparing one sibling to another can lead to a fixed mindset. The thought, "I will never be as good as my brother is at this, so why bother," is common when siblings are compared. No child is the same. They will each have their talents and interests. Let them be different.

THE WAY PARENTS JUDGE THEMSELVES

Adults like to say things like "I can't cook" or "I am terrible at crossword puzzles, so I don't try." Even if you don't mean any harm by saying these things, your children can hear you.

Keep a growth mindset and a positive attitude about yourself, just as you do for your child.

Remind yourself to forgo using the word can't. You can cook, just may not like to. Some people may be better than you. That is okay. You may cook something that turns out terrible or burnt. Treat your kids to take out that night, but be proud that you tried. Think about what you learned when you attempted that meal. Talk about it with your children, so they understand that you made an attempt and learned from it.

Now you are in a growth mindset about yourself. You may not ever be a great cook, but you have grown and learned along the way.

TAKE THE HARDER PATH

As I talked about in chapter 2, the growth mindset covers more than just academia. Friendships, sports, and other extracurricular activities can be as tricky as school assignments.

Succeeding at school is much easier than succeeding at things requiring more emotion, like friendships or interacting with strangers. Since these things are more complicated than math or reading, your child must put in all the effort required to succeed in all aspects of life. There are no shortcuts.

One of the hardest things to overcome is watching someone else navigate more easily through difficult situations. Humans, children especially, tend to envy others with these talents. They wonder, "Why is it so easy for them and so hard for me?" or "What is wrong with me? Why can't I be more like the "popular" kids?"

The questions that you should ask in these situations are "Wow, how did they learn to do that so well?" or "I wonder how much work it took to be able to do that so well? I wonder if I can put in that much work too?"

Please encourage your children not to envy their peers but work harder to become more like those they admire.

5

HOW TO STRENGTHEN GRIT IN OUR CHILDREN

Certain personality traits emerge when children and adults have a growth mindset. One of these traits that are starting to be researched is grit.

I first heard the term grit used to describe some athletes as a child. I was never really sure what it meant, though. I assumed it had something to do with strength or roughness. I came to this conclusion because the only other time I heard the word was to describe the roughness of sandpaper or the bits of sand on a beach.

If I had decided to look up the word grit when I heard it in middle school, I would have found the definition in my 1995 Webster's dictionary to be "stubborn courage, pluck." But, instead, my college dictionary added the words "brave perseverance" to the definition of grit.

Now there is a more refined definition of grit that some researchers are using.

Angela Duckworth came up with this definition, "Grit is the perseverance and passion for achieving long-term goals." Since then, several other researchers have studied grit. For example, James Clear refers to grit as "mental toughness." Mental toughness goes along with my junior high definition of "stubborn courage" (Duckworth, 2013).

In the context of the growth mindset, we use James Clear's definition. But, unfortunately, the dictionary definitions left out the most critical aspects of what grit is. The previous description gets closer by adding "brave perseverance," but it still doesn't go far enough (Clear, 2016).

According to Duckworth, the part that says "to achieve long-term goals" is the most critical aspect of what grit truly is. People who have grit are more likely to be successful regardless of their IQ or talent. This is not a new theory, though, and it has been underrated for many years. The idea of perseverance and tenacity have been considered to be necessary since the days of Aristotle.

Angela Duckworth is a researcher at the University of Pennsylvania and began researching grit when she started teaching 7th-grade math in New York City's public school system. In her first year of teaching, she began to notice that the kids doing the best in her class were not the best or the brightest. As her teaching career continued, she began to see that this was not a fluke. This trend of who performed the best in class was not always the students with the highest IQ.

In her 2013 TED Talk, she concludes that schools needed to look at education and learn from a different perspective (Duckworth, 2013). She felt the schools should measure things like student motivation from a psychological perspective rather than just IQ and standardized test scores.

To test her theory, she went to graduate school and became a psychologist. She and her fellow researchers went to places like West Point and the National Spelling Bee. They wanted to see if they could predict who would be successful. For example, who would stay in the rigorous West Point training program, and which kids would go the furthest in the spelling bee?

At West Point, recruits spend their first summer going through a grueling series of activities to make sure they are qualified to be officers. Duckworth compared how the new cadets ranked in school, how high their SAT scores were, leadership potential, physical aptitude, and grit level.

Her results showed that the cadets with the higher grit scores were the ones that did the best and completed the problematic summer training. Conversely, the other four categories she looked at figured into the cadets' success rate at a much lower level than grit.

She also studies first-year teachers working in the roughest schools to see who would make it through the school year. She even went to major sales companies to predict when sales reps would be the most successful.

She and her team discovered that the one thing all of the successful people had in these very different settings wasn't IQ, or skill, or talent; it was grit. She put this idea that grit was a person's most important attribute to the test by going to Chicago public schools and measuring a grittiness to graduation ratio in students. Her data back up her theory. Grit is very valuable to children and adults in correlation to achieving those long-term goals the definition talks about.

When Angela Ducksworth made her TED Talk, there had been little research done on how some people had more grit than others. But she credited a growth mindset as being a precursor to grit.

A fixed mindset tells you that you are the best you can be with the talents you were born with. This mindset will make it very difficult to have the motivation to achieve a long-term goal.

The growth mindset, however, naturally builds motivation and determination. In addition, it shows that failure is temporary. Angela wasn't sure how grit developed, but she did know that a growth mindset was the first step in getting there.

TRAITS OF MENTAL TOUGHNESS OR GRIT

Margaret M. Perlis, a contributor to Forbes magazine, has challenged the use of "to achieve long-term goals" as part of Duckworth's definition of grit. She argues that people with grit may not focus on long-term goals, but this doesn't disqualify them from being gritty. She asserts the grit is more about a person or child's attitude, not about achieving a goal at some unknown time in the future (Perlis, 2013).

Angela Duckwork did her research based on the parameters of educational achievement. Therefore, she had to use educational data such as standardized test scores and grade-level outcomes. We know that she did some research in the corporate setting as well. However, that research too was based on long-term results, not achievements accomplished daily.

I agree with Pelis in her assessment that grit can be seen in those who are not looking at the big picture of success in the future. This area of grit and mental toughness can be seen in firefighters. They are tasked with putting out fires. There is no long-term goal in fire fighting. They are not sitting around studying how to combat fires while waiting for a massive forest fire.

Firefighters have to use their grit to make rapid decisions. Duckworth spoke about massive life-altering events that will show us a person's grit, and one could argue that fire fighting fits into that category. In reality, most fires are not life or death situations. We only hear about the big ones because they make the news. Firefighters have grit simply because they are willing to put themselves in a dangerous situation every day.

This analogy leads me to the five traits that lead to grittiness.

Trait 1: Courage

In the news, we hear a great many "feel good" stories about people who did some extraordinary courageous thing that helped change someone's life. That is well and good. I love those stories, but that is not the whole picture of courage.

When I was in college, I read a lot! But one of the few things that stuck with me was one single line from Alexander Pope's "An Essay on Criticism." It is "For fools rush in where angels fear to tread." Many people have quoted that line in various situations. In the essay's context, it had to do with certain people being overly critical about something they have no business criticizing.

But, in the four hundred years since Alexander wrote that line, it seems to have morphed into a treatise on doing foolish things. But I look at that line differently. I hear it as a tongue-in-cheek comment about courage. After all, the most courageous acts are of someone running into a tricky situation when no one else will. People with a great deal of courage rush in where everyone else fears to tread. Some people have called courageous acts foolish. Maybe they are. But when the irrational rush in to help in rough spots, no one else complains.

For children, courage is hard to see. They know it as foolish rushing it to danger because that version of courage is what stories, books, and movies depict.

As a parent, you should change the way your child understands courage. It can be a heroic act, but it can also be an everyday act of overcoming fear and doing "foolish" things, and being foolish enough to stand up to the playground bully even though it may cause them some physical pain. They are foolish enough to help an older adult in distress and being stupid enough to be in the school play even though messing up could be humiliating. They are being foolish enough to overcome fear to do the right thing and being foolish enough to pick themselves up and move on after a literal or figurative fall. And yes, to be stupid enough to rush in where angels fear to tread because, unlike those wise angels, the child can overcome the fear and do what the wise angels could not.

Trait 2: Conscientiousness

One of the definitions I read about conscientiousness defines it as "a desire to do a task well and conscientious people are efficient and organized, not resting until the job is done and done right … They like the appearance of orderliness and tidiness and are good organizers, catalogers, and list makers." (The South African College of Applied Psychology, 2019) This is part of conscientiousness for some people. Not all conscientious people are that organized.

I went back to my trusty dictionary to get the official definitions. "1) Done according to what one knows to be right; upright; honest. 2) Showing care and precision; painstaking" Definition 1 is the definition that leads to grit.

Many children ignore things happening in the world. Instead, they see what is in their immediate vicinity. Some of them have no idea how to be conscientious because they don't need to know what is right. They know not to steal or pull their sister's hair, but many have convictions about the world outside of their bubble.

I was a very conscientious child, and my parents were beneficial to me. I remember seeing on the news the day Nelson Mandela was released from prison in South Africa. I was about 10 or 11, and I didn't understand why one man getting out of jail in another country was newsworthy. I asked my parents what it meant. They could have told me that I was too young, and they would explain it to me when I was older, but they did not do that. Instead, they sat me down at the dining table and explained who Nelson Mandala was, what apartheid was, and the significance of these things to the rest of the world. I didn't understand parts at that age, but I came to understand the importance later.

Later on, in college, a friend was talking about the Dave Matthews Band and that she had just found out that Dave Matthews was born in Johannesburg, South Africa. She mused about how nice it must have been and wondered why he would have left. I explained to her that he would have been living there during apartheid. She had no idea what I was talking about. She didn't know who Nelson Mandala was. As the conversation continued, I realized that nearly everyone at the gathering was looking at me as if I was telling a wild story about the distant past.

I was shocked at how no one had been conscientious about the world around them. It had only been ten years since Mandela's release. Through further inquiries, I found out that several of my friends had heard of Nelson Mandela, but their parents shielded them from the hard truth of what went on in South Africa.

As a parent, don't "protect" your children from bad or scary things happening in the country or world. Part of building grit is to understand the world and for them to know what is right. Children must have an understanding of "the right thing to do or be" to meet the first definition of conscientiousness; "done according to what one knows to be right; scrupulous; honest." They must form an idea of scruples.

Conscientious children will ask questions and, with honest answers, will form their idea of what the right thing to do.

A great example of a teenager with grit formed from conscientiousness is Greta Thunberg. She is an activist on climate change. She is not 18 but has been doing climate activism for several years now. Whether you agree with her or not doesn't matter. She has grit, and it started because she was conscientious about the climate.

Trait 3: Perseverance

Margaret M. Pelis concedes that though she doesn't like the part of the definition of grit that talks about long-term goals, succeeding at long-term goals is part of having grit for some people. Perseverance is a long-term ability.

Finishing a challenging homework assignment or rushing in to save the day doesn't require perseverance. To persevere, a person must be going through a long-term difficulty that they must overcome.

For children, that can be struggling with reading or math for more than a few weeks of dealing with the long-term ramifications of standing up to the playground bully. Perseverance can be challenging for a child to grasp. As parents and teachers, we like to tell children that they will learn if they keep trying, but do we ever really explain what perseverance is or talk about the coping skills needed to persevere through adversity?

Perseverance can be a very abstract concept. It is not tangible and, unlike courage, it is hard to point to because it is something done over time. So, when talking to your children about perseverance, have them think of different long-term difficulties. Then, once they have an idea of the difficulties, explain why they might give up or why they might stick it out and overcome the difficulty.

When going through a long-term situation, it gets harder for some children to keep going. So, helping them build excellent coping skills for difficult things will help them persevere through the tough times. Getting through a difficult situation with only a few bruises will lead to grittiness and that mental toughness they need.

Trait 4: Resilience

Resilience is being able to bounce back rapidly from a setback. As a teacher, I found that resiliency is a trait that comes more naturally to younger children. Adults work on a single path forward. So, a setback that knocks an adult off the course can make it hard to get back on the track.

Younger children tend to meander along several paths that all lead to the same outcome. A setback knocks them off of one track, so they go to the next one and shrug off the reverse.

Older children will need more help to be resilient. Approaching life with the ability to laugh or shrug things off is essential to resilience. As children get older, they get more serious about the world they live in. However, even with a more serious approach, being optimistic about their situation is imperative. Having a positive outlook on even the bleakest of conditions will make it easier to overcome, knowing that something positive is coming out of the difficulty.

Conscientiousness also plays a role in resilience. Children who have found their scruples and know what they believe to be accurate and right helps to keep them on the path. A setback isn't as significant a deal if they are sure they are doing the right thing. Self-awareness is also essential. Being aware of who they are helps the child be more flexible in difficult situations.

Getting up, dusting themselves off after a fall, and moving on is a sign of grit.

Trait 5: Passion

Loving what you are doing is vital to success in the short term and long term. The majority of the books on happiness and peace in life will maintain the most crucial aspect will be what you do for a living is the most critical aspect of finding peace. It also makes dealing with difficulties and setbacks easier because you love what you do, so the problems are worth it.

This adage is just as true for children. Kids who love reading will work harder to understand more complicated stories, even if it means looking up words they don't know. Likewise, children who are passionate about a particular sport will put in the hard work. They will deal with bumps and bruises and sore muscles because it is worth it to keep getting to do what they love. That is when their grit starts to set in.

Parents sometimes see their child's passion as silly or not productive. And, either on purpose or intentionally, some parents discourage emphasis in their children or steer them towards something more suitable to be the stereotypical version of success.

When I decided what to major in in college, my father discouraged me from majoring in English. He said, "you will have to marry an engineer, or you will starve to death." He simply didn't believe that I would be successful (make a lot of money) with an English degree.

My brother was already in college and majoring in marketing. But my brother was struggling. He wasn't passionate about all the math classes he needed to take.

Instead, he wanted to make money because he thought that would mean he was successful.

He graduated, got a job, and made the money he wanted, but he doesn't enjoy what he does. It is just a job to him. On the other hand, I have had an incredible journey as a writer and educator. I do not make as much money as my brother, but I love what I do. When things are difficult, I recover faster because I have a passion for what I do.

My mom encouraged me to be paramount in English because she saw my passion. She helped nurture my passion. She also felt that I wouldn't make a lot of money, but she understood that I had to do something I loved.

To have true grit, a child needs some of all of these treats. Of course, they will have varying levels of each, but they will have the components they need to build grit and mental toughness.

STRATEGIES FOR CREATING GRIT IN CHILDREN

James Clear used Angela Duckworth's research to create strategies for finding your grit. Mr. Clear uses the terms grit and mental toughness interchangeably (Clear, 2016).

In his research, he found that more than 70% of a person's achievements are based on their intelligence which matches that of Duckworth's studies. Grit is essential in all aspects of a person's life because we have more than one long-term goal in our lives.

It is excellent to know that grit will help your child succeed, but how does a person develop grit? Grit is not something a person is born with, like IQ or athletic abilities. It is something a person has to grow.

Clear's assessment of achieving mental toughness or grit is that a person needs to be consistent.

Athletes with grit are the ones who come to practice and their workouts and work hard to improve if they are not great at something. They are also willing to help their teammates if they play a team sport.

Business owners with grit always have their eyes on their goals. They don't get distracted by short-term setbacks, less than stellar feedback, or a packed calendar. Instead, they have a plan, and they keep going forward to reach the goal. They also tend to be positive and praise their colleagues for making everyone happier.

Workers with grit strive to meet their deadlines and accomplish their daily tasks. They take responsibility for their work and do their result whether they feel motivated or not.

It doesn't matter how talented your child is or isn't; they can develop their grit by having consistency.

Jame Clear recommends three ways you and your child can build grit.

1. Have your child figure out what grit is for them.

For those Westpoint students, grit and mental toughness are what are going to help them to make it through that grueling summer.

Mental toughness is different for everyone. Your child should think this through carefully.

Your child may see grit as needed to help them complete their homework assignments every day for a month before they watch tv or play video games.

It could be to do their chores every day without being asked to do them.

Maybe it is to stop drinking sugary sodas for a while or go for more walks at the park.

The goal needs to be a real-world action that your child can do realistically and consistently.

2. Grit is achieved through small successes.

Most people don't think about grit until there is a significant event that requires some toughness mentally and possibly physically. But, then, things like hurricanes, earthquakes, floods, fires, and other disasters test the average person's strength and perseverance.

This would be a championship game, the Olympics, the World Cup, Superbowl, or World Series for athletes. This is when we see what the world's best athletes are made of.

Most of the world's grit is being tested now with the COVID-19 pandemic. Finally, world leaders' true grit or lack thereof is displayed for all of humanity to see.

But the question remains, how did people develop this grittiness and mental fortitude? It doesn't just appear when something catastrophic happens.

Grit is developed over time. It requires daily practice and small victories every day. These victories are things like doing one more push-up when you are tired, jogging a couple of minutes longer when you feel like you are done, doing an extra math problem when your brain is tired, or practicing spelling words one additional time.

These things need to be done physically to sync up your child's body and their brain to work together to build up this mental grit over time

3. Grit is built through good habits, not motivation or willpower

Willpower can run out, and motivation is not always around when a child needs it. Creating grit within a child's growth mindset is about being motivated every day or having the willpower not to eat all the Oreos in one sitting. It is about creating good habits and routines. Once a child has a pattern or practice of doing something, it doesn't matter how motivated they feel or how much willpower they have on a given day. This routine will take over.

Creating grit doesn't require extreme talent, high intelligence, or even a lot of courage. All it takes is being consistent in the things your child does. To make a child mentally tough, they need to create a schedule or system to help them concentrate on the essential things that need to be achieved. This system will help them stay on track and be least susceptible to distractions or difficulties along the way.

These strategies are primarily for younger children. I will cover grit for teens in the next chapter.

DEVELOPING A GROWTH MINDSET WITH TEENS

When dealing with teenagers, some of the rules change because teenager's brains change as they reach puberty. As a result, some or all of the tactics and practices parents used for younger children need to be upgraded.

THE TEENAGE BRAIN

As teenagers reach puberty, their bodies start to change to prepare them for adulthood. Parents and teens alike see and somewhat understand these changes. However, parents and teens don't see that the brain also changes to prepare for the more complex needs of an adult.

Younger children tend to think in a very concrete way without really understanding the complexities of higher emotional thinking like sexuality, challenging friends, and the like. Children's brains don't need those sorts of thoughts.

As humans reach adulthood, the need for more abstract and higher emotional thinking becomes an integral part of success as an adult. In addition, adults need higher levels of problem-solving skills that go beyond the concrete world around them.

To make these more abstract thoughts accessible, the brain has to tear down some of its older structures and rebuild new ones. While this process is happening, more than just the way a teenager thinks is affected. Emotions are also involved because the capacity to build stronger and more complex relations is also needed for adulthood.

This new construction in the brain causes teens to be more irrational, have less ability to control impulses, take more risks, and make them want to push the limits of their boundaries.

With a teen's brain under construction, the strategies used for cultivating and maintaining a growth mindset have to be changed or tweaked to work. Unfortunately, many teens fall back into a fixed mindset simply because the new connection in their brains has stripped away some of the older ideas that help them remain positive and open to growth.

There will still be struggles for who should have all the power, but with strategies, parents can make it easier for themselves and their teen to navigate a brain under construction.

With a growth mindset, these struggles can be more manageable.

GROWTH MINDSET STRATEGIES FOR TEENS

Here are some strategies given by the writers of Big Life Journal (biglifejournal.com, 2017).

Teach how the brain works

In school children and teens, teach about the parts of the brain and what each piece does. Students hear words like the prefrontal cortex, limbic system, frontal lobe, synapse, and neurons, but that is where most knowledge of the brain stops unless a kid is interested in neuroscience.

Most average people do not understand the complexities of the brain. I have learned about how the brain works through research for this book and research into better ways to work with my group of adults with intellectual disabilities.

It stands to reason that the average teen does not know that their brain is changing or how those changes will affect them as they become adults.

Teaching them what is happening in their brains will help them understand that is brain construction and what is happening to them is temporary. It also helps them to make better decisions about their mindset.

Teach your teen more in-depth details about the parts of the brain and what they do. For example, teach them about neuroplasticity and how that is important to growth and memory.

Some good websites can help you with this. I will get to more information about these resources in chapter 9 where there will be a tool kit of resources available for you.

Never stop talking about it

The conversations relating to growth mindset should become part of the "dinner table" conversations. Discuss growth mindset whenever possible, but don't force things on your teen or they will just tune you out.

Look for examples of growth and fixed mindsets in everyday life such as in tv shows or books, even in Shakespeare. Then, compare the characters with growth and fixed mindsets. See who fares better and why.

Talk to your teens about your struggles with a growth mindset when you were their age and up to the present. What obstacles were there for you? How did you overcome them? In the period of COVID-19, we have all had to learn new ways to work and play. Make these new methods the focal point of growth mindset conversations.

It will help them to see that you understand a bit of what they are going through even though your brain is now fully built.

No pressure, just goals

Some teenagers aspire to live on Mars while others just want to pass English I or Algebra II.

Some teens may struggle with what goals they should set for themselves or how to go about setting concrete, attainable goals. In this case, it becomes easy to steer them in the direction you as their parents want them to go in.

Allow your teen to discover what they want on their own. Then, once they set the goals, concentrate on their work towards them more than achieving them, especially if your child's goal is to help colonize Mars.

Let failure in

Bring failure into your lives. Some parents feel that protecting their teen from failure is the best way to keep them happy, but life is messy. They will have failures as adults with no one to shield them.

Some teenagers are more emotional when they fail than younger children. As a parent, your role is to comfort your teen. Show them the ways to learn from failure. Make it clear this isn't the end of the world as long as they know and continue moving forward.

Work together to solve issues as they arise

When your teen fails or an obstacle occurs, help them decide the best path to take. Instead of telling them what to do, like asking the teacher if they can retake the test, give your teen a chance to weigh their options. Help them decide their own best course of action.

Fill in the skills gaps

As we discussed earlier, teens sometimes struggle with anxiety and depression due to their changing brain chemistry and other factors like lack of coping skills.

Puberty brings in a whole new set of emotions that your teen hasn't experienced before. With experience comes the need for new skills or improvements on old ones.

If your teen is struggling with anxiety or depression, seek out ways to help them. Do not blow it off, just get over it, or that it wasn't that big a deal. Unfortunately, their under construction brain often will not allow them to "just get over it."

Listen more and talk less

As a parent, you were a teenager once, so you know a lot about what it was like for you. You have a lot that you can share with your teen; however, it just sounds like you are lecturing them in most cases. No one likes being talked about things they already know or can figure out on their own.

Let your teen lead the conversations. Ask them questions that are not a simple yes or no. Get them to think about what to do. This builds their problem-solving skills and grows and strengthens their brains.

Listen to what they have to say, but let them draw their conclusions. Then, impart your wisdom in small amounts where it will be the most impactful to the conversation.

Be aware of your reactions

Sometimes you as a parent have a lot going on. So when your teen comes to you with an issue, make sure you operate in your positive growth mindset.

If you fly off the handle over something that is not very serious, then your teen will not be willing to come to you with more complex challenges, leading to more severe consequences.

Use a calm voice when you have to remind your teen that mistakes and failures will happen. A lot of the time, depending on the infraction, your teen has already punished and fussed at themselves enough for the both of you.

HOW TO MAKE GRITTIER TEENS

Helping your teenager become grittier is a little more complicated than a younger child or an adult due to those differences in their brains. It has to be more of a group effort. Parents have to play a part in creating the grittiness of their teens.

Create and keep a positive relationship

It is not easy to raise a teenager. Boundaries get pushed or even broken. Many have an attitude you don't like and friends you don't trust. While these things should certainly be addressed as needed, also focus on the positives.

A few years into my teaching career someone came up with Positive Behavior Interventions and Supports

(PBIS). The concept was to catch students doing the right thing and rewarding them to encourage other students to show positive behavior. Not only did this work pretty well with encouraging better behavior in others, but it also, in many cases, created a good rapport with teachers and the kids with middle-of-the-road behaviors.

This is the same concept as a parent of a teen or teens. Praise and reward them for doing something right. Even though this is expected behavior and what they should be doing, reward them anyway. It doesn't have to be large or extravagant, maybe just a simple, "Thanks for helping me set the table." or "Nice job with helping your little brother feed the dog." Make sure they know that you noticed that they were doing the expected behavior.

Also, spend time with them on their terms. If they want you to watch a show with them, watch the show, even if you hate it. If they initiate the conversation, engage with them. The more positively they feel the more grittiness they get.

Lead your teen to what they love

Many teens these days want to be good at everything and they want everyone to like them. Unfortunately, no one is good at everything. Help your teen find one or two things they are passionate about and have them nurture those passions.

Some teens don't have anything they love. That is okay. Show them different things they might enjoy, but be careful not to expose them to something because you want them to love it.

Passion builds grit. Always support your teen's desire.

Put growth in the center

Sometimes you may need to remind your teen of how their brain works. Then, when things get complicated, they need to keep working at it. This will strengthen the neurons in that particular skill set.

Building grit is more about the process than the results. Notice I didn't say the result. With a growth mindset and a good amount of grit, there is no result. The results will continue to change as your teen builds better skills.

Be supportive without lowering your expectations

Keep high expectations for your teen and, with some grit, they will rise to your expectations. But make sure you help and encourage them to meet those expectations. For example, if they have a passion for a particular sport, help them excel. If they don't feel up to going to practice one day, remind them of the importance of their commitment to themself and their teammates. Then show up to their games and be excited for them whether they win or lose.

Grit is not built by winning all the time; it is made by working to get better even if they don't win a championship.

Be an example of grit

Choose gritty behaviors yourself. Start a conversation with your teen about some difficulties you are having at your job. Step out of your comfort zone a bit and try new things to strengthen your neurons.

Your teen is what you are, they will follow your pattern of behavior. If you build grit, so will they. If you choose not to develop your grit, they will feel they don't need to do it either.

Read up on the teenage brain

We have already covered what is happening to your teenager's brain, but it was a small summation of what is going on in their brains. So do your research, and share it with your teen.

Create goals and routines

I mentioned earlier that some teens set impressive long-term goals for themselves. That is great, but to build grit, your teen needs attainable goals. For example, if they want to be the first astronaut on Mars, start with passing a calculus test. Then, once that test is passed, set a new goal.

Make the work toward these goals a routine. If it requires an hour of extra studying to understand the math, then build that extra hour into your teen's day. Motivation and willpower are not always present while the teen brain is under construction. Things must then become a habit so they will get done.

Develop gratefulness

A positive attitude leads to grit, and gratitude leads to a lot of positivity. So ask your teen about things they are thankful for, share your joys and thankfulness with them.

Model grateful behavior in public settings but also to your teen. You are thrilled that they are doing so well. They might say you are embarrassing them, but they are glad to know you are grateful for them. They will have a more positive outlook and that is where they will find their grit.

Let them fall, but help them up

Many parents don't like to see their kids hurt. But letting teens fall and get scraped up a bit is necessary.

So help them up and give them a bandaid, but make them learn from this fall. First, they will know that they lived through whatever the metaphorical fall was, and second, they will learn not to do that again.

About a year after I got my driver's license, I wrecked my car on my way to school. I was not far from home. When a neighbor arrived on the scene with my mother she hugged me. Then she asked me what happened. I told her the stupid thing I had done. She responded by saying, "Well, I guess you will never do that again. This is how we learn." I also had to ride the school bus to high school until I could afford another car.

That situation was difficult for me, but I have been a more careful driver ever since. I also learned the consequences of not having a car. If my mom had gotten another vehicle right away, I may not have learned she could not rescue me as an adult.

You want your teen to learn how to deal with difficulties while supporting them with ways to cope with the test. Once they leave home, they have to be gritty enough to solve their problems.

Use grit for the greater good

Grit is also forged by the passion and drive to help others. To have grit your teen needs to do things that go beyond just their wants and needs.

After you have found your teens' passion, help them turn the things they love into creative ways to help others.

GROWTH MINDSET AND TEEN STRESS

Middle and high school can be a mind field of emotions and stress. On top of keeping up with academics, there is drama with friends, and trouble with mean students. With a brain being slowly reconstructed, it is difficult to believe that these things will pass.

Having a growth mindset will help your teen deal with stress better than those with a fixed mindset. What is clear is that the way the growth mindset is framed makes a difference too.

Psychologists at the University of Texas at Austin and the University of Rochester did a study to see if a slight change in mindset would change the stress levels of high school students (Wheeler, 2016).

They chose 60 high school students and gave them a 30-minute lesson on growth mindset. Thirty of the students were taught about a growth mindset from an emotional standpoint.

They learned that being left out is okay. They were shown that no one is inherently bad and that everyone is capable of change. Thirty of the students were taught about growth mindset from an emotional standpoint. The other 30 students were taught about growth mindset also but from a physical perspective. They learned how to deal with new lockers and how to navigate new hallways.

The group that learned a growth mindset from the emotional side of things did better overall in high school.

7

GROWTH MINDSET VS. SPORTS PERFORMANCE

Mindset in sports could be the single most crucial thing to make or break an athlete's career.

There are a lot of people out there who would likely disagree with that statement. They would say that talent, or the lack thereof, is what makes or breaks an athlete's career. I have heard coaches say things like "This kid is going to be great. He has a gift" or "Well, he tries, but the talent just isn't there."

In her book, Dr. Dweck explains just how dangerous it is for young athletes to be told they will be significant because of how gifted they are or athletes won't be good at a particular sport because they aren't as talented as others (Dweck, 2006).

Dweck talks about several different athletes, some who were very talented and some who had to work very hard to make it to the top.

John McEnroe, who was a gifted tennis player, told Dweck how much he hated playing tennis. He loved the fame and fortune that came with winning, but because of his fixed mindset about his talents, he would fall apart if he lost. John found ways to blame other people and once even his shoes for losing. He believed that because of his talent he should win all the time and if John lost he was a failure. His fixed mindset kept him from understanding that he just needed to practice a little more to correct the mistakes he made when he lost.

Billy Bean was also a natural-born athlete. He played three sports in high school and excelled at all of them. He was once described as "the next Babe Ruth," but he too had a fixed mindset. Because of his talents, he never learned how to fail. So when he failed at something, he completely fell apart. For example, if he didn't get a base hit when he was at bat, Babe believed he was a failure.

Billy Bean played with another much less talented player named Lenny Dykstra. Bean is quoted as saying about Dykstra "He had no concept of failure ... And I was the opposite." (Dweck 2006) Bean watched as

Dykstra practiced every day and worked very hard to be good at baseball. The difference in their mindsets became very obvious to Bean who, as a general manager of the Oakland A's in 2002, began to look for players like Dykstra. He knew that he wanted players who worked hard to be better than their naturally talented counterparts.

Dweck talks about other players that were less talented but put in the work to become great. Micheal Jordan was taken off the varsity team in high school, and he was not recruited by the college team he dreamed of playing for. Why? Because, at the time, he was not the best player out there. He was tall and had some skills, but he simply wasn't good enough at the time. He worked harder and harder. He practiced the skills that were the weakest and he got better.

Micheal Jordan had a growth mindset. He believed that if he worked hard enough he would get better. However, he may not be considered the best basketball player ever played had he relied on natural talent.

Babe Ruth was not built to play baseball. Ballplayers at the time could have been hired to be the Macy's Department Store Santa in the off-season, but he had more of a Santa look than a ballplayer look. But Babe Ruth loved playing baseball and he worked very hard to be good at it. Babe Ruth also had the advantage of working on his hitting while he was a pitcher for the Boston Red Socks. Back then, and even to this day, pitchers were not expected to be great hitters. So, while he played for Boston, he could do whatever he wanted to at the plate to see what worked. By the time he was sold to the Yankees, he understood the need to work hard to improve his hitting.

Dweck goes on to give several other examples of great athletes who were not born with outstanding talent. All of whom had a growth mindset that allowed them to excel at their given sport.

The growth mindset leads to character and heart. Character in the sports world is usually used to describe a team player that does well because they are faced with adversity either within the sport itself or, in the case of the 2006 New Orleans Saints football team, significant adversity from Mother Nature herself. Thus adversity usually leads to resilience and grit. Heart is a player or team that plays with all the effort they can give even when faced with significant adversity.

In 2005, Hurricane Katrina badly damaged the level system along Lake Pontratrain leading to widespread flooding throughout New Orleans. For the 2005 football season, the Saints were unable to play a home game in New Orleans. They went 3-13 in that season.

The Saints hired a new coach named Sean Payton and a new quarterback named Drew Brees. Along with Drew Brees, the Saints put together a team of guys no one had heard of. Many of them were considered washed-up or young players who were not standouts in college. Drew Brees himself was coming off of shoulder surgery and there was a widespread belief that his career was over.

That 2006 team worked hard in the off-season to be a great team. They wanted to bring back hope to a devastated city. Drew Brees was especially keen on winning games. So new Orleans took a chance on him when no other team would.

The character of that 2006 team, which had a winning season for the first time in a long time, gave hope and joy to New Orleans when they needed it the most.

Sean Payton and Drew Brees both had growth mindsets, believing that they could be better than the sports analysts thought they could be with a lot of hard work and some creativity. That growth mindset was taught to the rest of the team. As a result, the Saints started winning, leading up to a 2009 SuperBowl victory. That show of character and heart-led many residents of New Orleans to declare their city as being cured of the heartache caused by a breached levee 4 years earlier.

Even with their best talents, players with a fixed mindset don't generally have character or heart. However, they do develop the resilience needed for heart and character because they rarely face adversity. When they do, they don't believe they can do anything about the adversity.

HOW TO DEVELOP A GROWTH MINDSET IN YOUNG ATHLETES

Dr. Dweck talks about many athletes with natural talent and athletes that work very hard to be great. However, she doesn't give examples of very talented athletes that also have a growth mindset.

This isn't to say that none exist, however. If your child has a natural talent make sure to instill a growth mindset to keep them from the same fate as Billy Bean and John McEnroe. Your child must understand that hard work is still necessary for being an athlete even if things come quickly to them. There will be a day when things don't come as quickly. They must be prepared for less than perfection.

The Big Life Journal offers advice about raising a growth mindset-oriented athlete. They give 5 effective strategies with a breakdown for each one.

Persuade Your Child to Try New or Different Activities

Most children prefer to do what they are good at. This applies not only to sports but to most things. If your child is good at one sport they may be afraid to try another one if they aren't as good at the other one.

Talk to them about the advantages of learning to play more than one sport. The skills they learn from one sport can carry over to another. Also playing a sport they are new to or not as skilled at will help them understand the necessity of hard work. And it shows them that they can improve at a new sport which helps to solidify the growth mindset concept that learning to improve is achievable.

Implement Angela Duckworth's "Hard Things Rule." Duckworth and her family pick a hard thing to do, like learning a musical instrument, playing a new sport, or even doing an inappropriate activity. Then, each family member chooses their own difficult thing and they are not allowed to quit (biglifejournal.com, n.d.).

This may sound like a crazy thing to make your family do, but they also must encourage each other along the way. The goal of the "Hard Things Rule" isn't to be good at something complicated, but to learn how to work to get better at something while helping to encourage and inspire the people around you.

As you learn this hard thing, talk about the joy and excitement doing new things can bring. Don't hide the difficulties, however. Instead, share the whole journey with your child and ask them to share their journey with you.

If they are scared to learn something new, ask them why. Be ready to help them work through this fear. Explain to them that they currently love to do were once new to them and you.

Promote steadfastness

Often, a child hears about a new sport that looks cool or a sport their friends are playing and want to play. So, you sign them up only to have them want to quit a little later when things get tough. Maybe they aren't as good as their friends, perhaps the sport requires skills they haven't mastered yet, or perhapsthey just changed their minds.

Before you sign them up for something new, talk about the word commitment. Talk about what it means and what it looks like. For example, part of Angela Duckworth's rule is that she and her family members cannot quit, because they are committed to the hard thing they are doing.

Point out that if they are on a team, quitting would hurt the team, even if they think they are not contributing to the team. Everyone brings something to make the team better.

Plan in advance solutions to any issues that may come up. Gabriele Oettingen, a professor of psychology at New York University, researches the impact of setting goals. She came up with the WOOP method to help stick to your or your child's dreams (biglifejournal.com, n.d.).

WOOP stands for Wish, Outcome, Obstacle, Plan. The wish is the goal your child is setting. An example might be to make the high school soccer team as a forward. The outcome is the best possible result to the wish or goal. An example would be to make the team bold and score the most goals on the team. The obstacle is what might stand in their way of achieving that goal. One example would be that they are not as fast as some of the other players on the team or have trouble getting the ball when it is passed to them. The plan is how they can work on fixing the obstacle in advance. For example, maybe they see that running a long time is a problem, so they plan to work on their endurance.

The WOOP method helps your athlete see that there may be issues along the way, but if they plan for it and are ready to deal with the problems, they will be less likely to want to quit.

What if you weren't able to impress upon them that they weren't allowed to quit before you signed them up? Then you can talk about how hard work and perseverance lead to outstanding accomplishments. No one is a success overnight.

Big Life Journal and others say to use the "Iceberg analogy." Dr. Dweck alludes to this idea in her book. She talks about athletes like Muhammad Ali. When he first started he was built to be a boxer and his technique was all wrong. Now that we know how good he was, people see him as a great example of what a fighter should be.

All we see now is the part of the iceberg that is on top of the water. We didn't see the characteristics of the Ali iceberg that were under the water. All the training and studying he did to become great. The same goes for most great athletes. All your child sees is what that athlete can do now. They don't see all the blood, sweat, tears, defeats, failures, grit, and effort into becoming an elite athlete.

Discuss those famous elite athletes your child idolizes. Then, do some research together to learn how that athlete got to where they are today. In nearly every case, you and your child will find some adversity that had to be overcome so the athlete could make it.

Even if your child decides that they still aren't in love with the new sport after a season, they will see that they made some progress because of their hard work and perseverance.

Redefine losing

Most children don't like to lose. They think that losing means they are a failure and bad at the sport they play.

Explain that losing or missing the critical catch or striking out doesn't make them bad at the game they are playing. Losing isn't failing, losing is an opportunity.

Losing can help a player or a team see their weakness and their strengths. After a loss, it is good to look back at what went wrong and what went well. Did your child improve from the previous game? When things went wrong, did they encourage other players?

Have them watch professional athletes, especially quarterbacks. After every possession, Drew Brees and other quarterbacks go back to the sideline and look back at the previous plays on an electronic tablet. Most of them do it after good possessions and bad ones. They do this to improve on their mistakes and help improve the mistakes of others so that once they are back on the field, they will do better.

The most important thing to impress upon your child is that win or lose the game should be fun. Unfortunately, sometimes children and even professional adults get so wrapped up in mistakes, and who has more points, that they forget that the point of playing any game is to have fun.

Redefine winning

The growth mindset is built and maintained through practice and hard work, not the result. So when your child or their team wins, praise them for how hard they work at practice. Show them that winning was a direct result of hard work and perseverance.

If winning was too easy for your child, then remind them that their win, though great, did not help them learn because there were few or no mistakes to know help them . Instead, it is the challenges that build the growth mindset and grit.

Show your child that constructive criticism is what makes them better

Most human beings do not like it when others are critical of how they do things, like a job, a sport, or a performance.

The word criticism has a negative connotation even when you put the word constructive in front of it. So, be careful to frame constructive criticism as friendly advice. Even elite athletes like Serena Williams or Usain Bolt have coaches who advise them about getting better.

Use your criticisms or advice strategically. Children will start to tune you out if you tell them too much at once. So instead, choose one or two things you feel need to work on and concentrate on those things. When they have mastered those skills, then work on more.

MODERN EXAMPLES OF ATHLETES WITH GROWTH MINDSETS

Dr. Dweck talks about several athletes in "Mindsets" that have growth mindsets. Here I will add to that list some new names that have become more household names since the 2006 publication of the book.

Molly Seidel

The first athlete I want to mention is Molly Seidel. Molly just won a bronze medal at the 2020 Olympic Games for running a marathon. Winning an award in the marathon event is a feat in itself. Seidel is only the 3rd American woman to win a medal in the Olympic

Marathon. The fact that this was only the third marathon she ever ran made it even more spectacular.

Seidel was a cross country athlete in high school and college. Cross country running is longer than most races (between 4-12 kilometers) and is run on grass through hills instead of a flat track.

Molly was a great runner in college at Notre Dame in Indiana. She was considered the fastest woman in the National Collegiate Athletic Association (NCAA). She mainly ran the 10-kilometer race (Gibson, 2020). In 2016, she was the Atlantic Coast Conference (ACC) female athlete of the year.

While she was in college, she began to struggle with an eating disorder. This disorder caused her to postpone her lifelong dream of going to the Olympics because she entered a treatment center instead.

After she left the treatment center, she started training again, but instead of the 10k race, she turned to marathon racing. She came in second in the 2019 Olympic trials, which was her first marathon. She thought the Olympics would be her second, but the Pandemic postponed the 2o2o Olympics for a year.

She used that extra year to train and run a marathon in London. She came in 6th but had a better time than the

Olympic trials. All of her hard work and struggling paid off when she won the Bronze medal.

She had a growth mindset. She knew that if she trained and put in the work she could get better. But it wasn't just her growth mindset. At the post-race interview from Japan, she revealed that her coach Jon Green (also a great runner) believed in her so much that he told her to bring her "podium uniform" just in case she won a medal. She thought he was nuts, but she brought it with her.

Molly had surrounded herself with family and friends with a growth mindset; all of them believed that she could work hard and train to win a 26 plus mile race, 20 miles longer than any race she had run before.

Tyrann Mathieu

Tyrann Mathieu was a very talented defensive football player at Louisiana State University in 2010 and 2011. In 2012 he was released from the team for breaking team rules. There were rumors that he had failed a few drug tests. Later that year he was arrested on drug possession charges.

Instead of giving up, Mathieu worked hard to get into shape and entered the 2013 NFL draft. He was signed and began a long and fruitful career in the NFL.

His growth mindset allowed him to overcome his college issue to become a great NFL player.

Michael Phelps

Michael Phelps is a household name. He has 28 Olympic medals in swimming, 23 of those are gold.

Michael began swimming when he was seven years old. His mother thought it was a good way for him to get rid of his massive amounts of energy. He and his sister decided they like swimming and decided to swim as a sport not just for fun.

A couple of years later, Michael Phelps' parents got divorced. The divorce impacted his mental health in very negative ways. He struggled with depression and was diagnosed with ADHD.

These obstacles taught him to work hard to be successful. He trained every day believing he could get better and better. His growth mindset led him to all of his medals, as well as the world records he broke.

He could have won on talent and his body shape, but he put in the extra hard work to go from good to great to the best in the world.

Bethany Hamilton

Bethany Hamilton, like most Hawaiians, loves to surf. She was on a surfboard at 3 years old. She began competitions at 8 and had a sponsor by 9 years old. This should be the end of her story, but it isn't, and it took a growth mindset for her story to go from being good at surfing to being great at surfing with a missing left arm.

On a typical October day in 2003 when Bethany was 13, she went surfing with her best friend and her best friend's father and brother. She was lying face down on her surfboard with her arms dangling in the water as she talked to her friend when her life changed forever.

A 14-foot long tiger shark mistook Bethany's left arm as a food source and attacked her. She was rushed to the hospital, but she lost her arm in the attack. After that, however, she set her mind on the idea that she would not stop surfing because of this.

In less than a month, she was back on a specially made surfboard to have better balance due to her missing arm. Soon after that, she was competing again. She has now learned to use a standard surfboard again.

Her experience led her to write a book about the shark attack and her return to the sport called "Soul Surfer.". She has written several other books based on her life and her Christan faith including "Be Unstoppable: The Art of Never Giving Up."

Never giving up is one of the best attributes of a growth mindset.

Sky Brown

Sky Brown is the youngest person to ever compete in the Olympics for Great Britain. She competed when she was only 13 years and 28days old. Her sport is skateboarding which made its Olympic debut at the 2020 Olympics.

She got into the sport because most of her family skateboards. She was able to start young because the preschool she went to had a skate park in it. She had many falls along the way, but she has a growth mindset so she kept getting back on her skateboard.

In July of 2021, while training for the Olympics, she fell from a halfpipe course. This was referred to as a horrific fall by several media outlets. She broke her wrist, hand and sustained a fractured skull in several places.

Despite almost dying, she competed in the Olympics, winning a bronze medal and winning gold at X-games.

All of these athletes had to overcome adversity to make it in their respective sports. But, if any of them had allowed a fixed mindset to make them give up when things got hard, we wouldn't know their names.

A-TEAM WITH A FIXED MINDSET

I have just talked about the greatness of some athletes with growth mindsets, but what happens if a team and its leaders have a fixed mindset?

In the 2017 baseball season, despite having a great team, the Houston Astro began using a video system to see the signs of the opposing team's catcher as he gave them to the pitcher. Once they had the signs they would use auditory signals to let the batter know what pitch was coming.

The Astro went to and won the World Series that season.

Sign stealing has always happened in baseball, but using a video camera is illegal in baseball.

The question remains why did they go to all this trouble to find out what pitch was coming next. This happened because the general manager had a fixed mindset about his team. He believed that the only way they could win was to cheat.

The sad thing is that the team was full of good hitters who may have hit well without knowing what pitch was coming. But the general manager had a fixed mindset and forced all of his players to have a fixed mindset about themselves. They believed that to be good hitters, they had to know what pitch was coming.

They were caught in 2018 and were sanctioned by Major League Baseball. After the cheating stopped, the team could still make it to the World Series in 2019, though they did not win it. The players must have changed their mindsets after the 2018 season to growth mindsets realizing they could still win games if they put in the work, without having to cheat.

8

GROWTH MINDSET IN WORK-- CASE STUDIES

Many businesses are beginning to see the advantages of implementing policies based on growth mindset practices. For example, Microsoft and Google have both discovered that growth mindsets increase productivity.

Google is even moving away from hiring only college graduates to their company. They have realized that many creative people can get on-the-job training and excel without a formal and prestigious degree.

In many of the case studies I read, companies are beginning to look for employees who believe that they can improve their skills as they move through the company. As a result, they are moving away from hiring brilliant people that think they already know the best way to do business.

If you are a parent with a child in their late teens, this information becomes vitally important. Your teen is either entering post-secondary education or the workforce.

With this shift in thinking about business, your child must be ready to enter this new workforce either right out of high school or after college.

Many colleges are beginning to use growth mindset strategies among their students and staff alike. Unfortunately, there is not much information on how to tell if a college culture has a growth or fixed mindset, but you and your teenager may be able to tell just by a campus visit. Many campuses will tell potential students their philosophies when they come to visit the campus.

Once they are ready to enter the workforce they need to be prepared for interview questions like this one used by Timothy Perlick the senior director of professional development at CME Group: "Describe a time you confronted a challenge. How did you work through it to overcome your doubts?" (Harvard Business Review, 2014).

Mr. Perlick says that his company doesn't necessarily hire just based on growth mindset-oriented questions, but it does help. Many companies have found that growth mindset-oriented employees tend to have more creative and unconventional ways of dealing with issues.

When looking for a job or a place for higher education, your teen should look for some or all of these traits in the work or school community.

These six traits were created from a case study of Barnert Temple in Franklin Lakes, New Jersey. Wendy Grinberg interviewed Rabbi Elyse Frishman and Rabbi Rachel Steiner and the Director of Lifelong Learning Sara Losch and five congregants to see how they could improve to make young people interested and re-engage with their faith (Grinberg, 2013).

The rabbis found the congregation needed change. So they used a growth mindset approach that helped bring about "...a new era that will offer all families a more accessible, relevant and meaningful Jewish experience." (Grinberg, 2013).

Trait 1: Community input, not a groupthink

Groupthink is the practice of thinking or making decisions as a group that discourages creativity or individual responsibility. The rabbi came into a stagnant synagogue and lost many young people to other things. It seemed like the Barnert Temple was using the process of groupthink to make decisions. Most decisions were based on the status quo. So, the rabbis both began to assess what changes needed to be made to change the status quo

When groupthink is going on, then everything revolves around the person in charge. If this had been a Fortune 500 company, the decision would fall to the CEO or a group of high-level managers. If this is the case at a large company, most of the company culture would make the CEO and his managers look good instead of making everyone look good.

These are the kind of places you want your teen to avoid. Instead, you want to find a place that takes the ideas of all the work or school community into account when planning or changing policies.

Trait 2: Various points of view

In most cases, a corporation or college cannot interview the entire workforce or student body. So, when they create a task force, it should have various experiences, cultures, and ideologies.

One of the rabbis at Barnert, Rabbi Frishman, explains why having a diverse point of view is essential in the decision-making process. She says "...if you invite the right people, they are going to have ideas that I haven't thought of." (Wendy Grinberg, 2013).

Trait 3: The higher-ups lead the way

Leaders with a growth mindset are the building blocks for a company with a growth mindset culture. In all of the case studies I read, the people at the highest levels began transforming companies from rewarding only a few "start" works to rewarding all workers for their efforts to improve the company.

The late Jack Welch, a former CEO of General Electric, liked to hire people from midwestern state schools that turned out people who understood the value of hard work or military vets. . He didn't like hiring graduates of Ivy League schools that were very intelligent but may have lacked an understanding of effort. Once he found the employees he wanted, he committed a lot of time training them. He believed that his employees could grow and become stars with the right effort.

Timothy Perlick credits the change in philosophy at CME Group to former CEO Bhupinder Gill in 2012. Gill came in with the belief that the business world was changing and becoming more globalized. He felt that employees need a growth mindset to come up with new innovative ways to conduct meaningful business in that changing world.

Gil believed in it so much that he hired Dr. Dweck to come in and train all the managers about growth mindsets. When this case study was done in November of 2014 by the Harvard Business Review, it was too early to tell if the growth mindset helped create more revenue for the company (Harvard Business Review, 2014). But Perlick said that the new mindsets helped establish better innovation techniques and were innovating much more rapidly.

Trait 4: Mistakes are teachable moments

When corporations have a growth mindset, they see mistakes as ways to learn. They won't blame individual employees. Many companies in the past and the present live by the philosophy that when mistakes happen or projects don't work, they say "we just learned how not to do that." This belief has always been a growth mindset perspective.

When you and your child are looking at schools or places where they may want to start a career, research how these places have dealt with mistakes that have happened. Look to see if setbacks lead to policy changes.

Companies with fixed mindset practices will not learn from their mistakes, leading to repeated mistakes and little growth among employees.

Trait 5: New adjustments are unceasing

Most people don't like change. This can be true for many companies as well. The members of Barnert Temple learned, with their new forward-thinking rabbi's way, that change and adjustments are inevitable if they want to stay relevant in a changing world. They also learned that changes can be a good thing; stagnation will never move forward.

Not only are changes inevitable for most companies, but they are necessary and constant. Therefore, growth mindset-oriented companies will thrive when challenges come up because they are ready to make the required changes to solve whatever their challenge may be.

In another case study I read, the author wrote about being aware of changing up a routine. First, however, he had to force himself to make the changes he needed to get his life headed in a better direction. Pushing himself from a fixed mindset to a growth mindset required changes in thinking and physical habits (Hunter, 2021).

Trait 6: Learning is continuous for all people

One of Dr. Dweck's professors, Seymour Sarason, emphasized questioning what people assume about our society. His example was about schools. When a person thinks of a school they feel about children going to learn. Sarason asked a question about why schools weren't also for teachers to learn as well.

He was onto something with that question, but it wasn't just as simple as teachers learning. I have heard people say things like I am done with school; I go to work now. There is this thought that once you are working, learning is no longer required. That is a fixed mindset belief. Companies should always offer their employees some sort of learning opportunity so the employees can improve their skills.

Doctors are required to renew their license every year to ensure they are learning new things about medicine all the time. Likewise, teachers have professional development training every year to ensure they use the latest innovations in education.

Always look for companies or organizations that train their employees as often as possible.

These are principles you and your teen should look for in companies and schools. If they find institutions that follow these principles, these principles will become a habit for your child. As a result, they will become better workers or students and happier at what they are doing.

9

A TOOL KIT FOR PARENTS

This chapter will go over some tools and best practice ideas for parents. As well as some of the tools used in writing this book.

COURSES YOU AND YOUR CHILD CAN PURCHASE OR DOWNLOAD FOR FREE

Mindworks

The Mindworks company developed growth mindset training courses based on Dr. Dweck's research and conclusions (*Growth Mindset Programs*, 2019).

These programs are curated for a particular age range. Different age groups have different cognitive function levels. The curriculum developers at Mindworks made three distinct and separate programs. The problems build off of the age level before it, but they can also be stand-alone courses.

If you have a teenager, then you need to start with the highest grade level program. However, beginning with one designed for younger children will not be beneficial. The highest level program will cover everything that needs to be learned. So, no need to start with the 1st program if it is not age-appropriate for your child.

Their program for pre-K to third grade is called GEMs which stands for Growing Early mindsets.

The next level program is for 4th - 8th graders. It is called Brainology for Home.

The last level program is for 9th - 12 grades. It is called Applied Brainology.

These programs, information about Dr. Dweck's research, as well as a helpful PDF about what to say and how to say it can be found on the Mindworks website mindsetworks.com

Big Life Journal

Big Life Journal has a lot of resources for kids in regards to mindset. Their website states they have over 500,000 positive youth using their journals.

They have divided their resources by ages 4-10 years old and 11 years old and higher. They also have printable resources like posters about famous people who succeed because of growth mindsets. Prices vary depending on what you want.

You can find them at BiglifeJournal.com

Cool Beans Living

Cool Beans Living has a program similar to Big Life Journal. Cool Beans Living urges you and your child to get rid of negative thoughts. They explain that without negative thoughts a person will be happier, healthier, and find more success. They emphasize how much a positive outlook can help improve a person's life.

This positivity can keep you healthy, help you deal with stress, and help you live longer. It will also help your child find positive people. Being around positive people will help your child make better decisions because they will have positive peer pressure.

Here is what they offer for 17.00 USD. Their toolkit includes 8 different components:

Guide to Positive Mindset, Guide to Positive Affirmations, Habit Tracker, Mindset Journal Prompts, Mindset Workbook, Daily Mindset Planner, Bullet

Journal, Motivation Posters. You can find this kit at CoolBeansLiving.com

Karen Allen

Karen Allen also has a good growth mindset toolkit. She believes that building a solid mindset starts with small daily habits. Karen Allen has put together several resources including tips, strategies, and practices, to help you and your child cultivate a positive mindset.

She feels that using these resources will help a person create a better life and see firsthand how important mindset is.

On her website karenallen.co/toolkit you will find:

10 Mental Blocks & 20 Positive Mindset Shifts

"Thinking traps are patterns of thought - usually with a negative slant - which prevent us from seeing things as they are. These positive shifts will help you balance emotions with logic so you can show up fully with hope, optimism, and joy."

50 Self-Care Ideas

"Mindfulness is not just meditation, trips to the spa, and yoga (even though all of those ideas are great habits!). This download is just a long list of ideas and includes some of my favorite, easy, fun self-care ideas."

5-day Digital Detox

"Stepping away from your screens will benefit your mindset, your quality of life, and your relationships. Take a break from technology and create healthy boundaries that help you disconnect from the world so you can reconnect with yourself and your loved ones."

51 Mental Strength Training Exercises

"Mental health is not only about mental disorders and illnesses, but it's also about mental strength training so your mind is flexible, alert, and focused on growth."

These are all free to download. She also has "The Ultimate Guide to Living Fully and Feeling Whole" This workbook will help you and your child get through the tough stuff in life.

This guide includes:

- 10 life-hacks to help you break through obstacles that have been holding you back from building a life you love.
- Exercises, questions, and planners to help you make positive changes and finally take control of your life.
- Tips for getting into a positive mindset that attracts abundance and growth.
- Action steps to clarify your priorities and create

more mindful routines to help you make good decisions and achieve your goals.
- Activities and prompts to help you declutter your mental space and cultivate more peace, joy, and balance on your terms.
- You need all of the guidance to create a resilient foundation that will support you through all of life's ups and downs.

At the time of the publication of this book, the price of "The Ultimate Guide to LivingFully and Feeling Whole" is down from $24 to $12 (Allen, n.d.).

Positive Change Guru

Positive Change Guru has a great toolkit as well. The Introduction to Growth Mindset is a free course. This is what it includes:

- learn more about mindset
- understand the impact mindset has on you and those around you
- appreciate how mindset can develop or bury potential

The course is delivered into three modules:

1. What is mindset?

2. How to recognize a growth mindset and fixed mindset
3. Beginning your growth mindset journey

Let's dive straight into this Introduction to Growth Mindset course which will equip you with all the tools you need to begin your growth mindset journey. In this course you will:

- get to grips with the basics of the growth mindset.
- take time to reflect on how mindset has influenced different areas of your life until now.
- consider the areas in which you'd like to expand your growth mindset.

BOOKS THAT ARE GREAT RESOURCES

Two books recommended by other writers are Ken Ginsburg's "Raising Kids to Thrive: Balancing Love with Expectations and Protection with Trust" and Jessica Lahey's "The Gift of Failure: How the Best Parents Learn to Let Go So Their Children Can Succeed"

"Raising Kids the Thrive" answers two questions: 1. How do I give my child the unconditional love he needs to thrive, while also holding him to high expectations?

2. How do I protect my child while also letting her learn life's lessons? (Raising Kids to Thrive, n.d.). Both of these questions are concepts that have been touched throughout this book.

"The Gift of Failure" explores why it is important to let children learn from their failures. Learning from failure is an integral part of having a growth mindset. This book may help you find a better mindset about watching your child fail. It is difficult to watch someone we love fail at something they enjoy. This book thoroughly explains why letting your child fall is so important.

James Clear writes about mental toughness. He wrote the book "Atomic Habits: An Easy and Proven Way to Build Good Habits and Break Bad Ones." This is a book all about creating good habits. Good habits are part of maintaining a growth mindset. Mr. Clear also has what he calls 3-2-1 Thursday emails. He gives you 3 ideas, 2 quotes, and 1 question to think about each week. You can sign up for these emails at JamesClear.com/newsletter. The newsletter is growth mindset and mental toughness oriented.

Of course, the basis for all of this is Dr. Dweck's book "Mindset: A New Psychology of Success." You can purchase this book in hardcover for less than $20. Mindset has a lot of anecdotal stories from Dr. Dweck's journey researching mindsets. Her journey from a fixed mindset to a growth mindset helps her readers understand how this groundbreaking research came to be. For example, Dr. Dweck credits her 6th-grade teacher for putting the students in order by their IQ levels as the catalyst for her fixed mindset. Later, she questioned if IQ level was the only way to rate a child from an educational standpoint.

This is not an endorsement or recommendation of these programs. However, this information is included in this book so that you as a parent know some of the options you have if you wish to continue your child's learning of growth mindsets outside of the scope of this book.

CONCLUSION

The main takeaway from this book is that a person's mindset can be life-changing. As a parent, you want what is best for your child. Teaching them to have and maintain a growth mindset could be the most critical thing you teach your child. Giving them the gift of a growth mindset will set them up to be lifelong learners with the confidence to follow their dreams. They will understand that hard work and perseverance will help them succeed at whatever they put to their mind.

A growth mindset will help your child increase the number of dendrites and synapses they grow while they strengthen neurons in their brain, leading to higher intellectual intelligence and emotional intelligence. These two traits will ultimately lead to a happier and healthier life.

Keep in mind that this is a process and will not happen overnight. It takes a great deal of commitment and hard work to maintain a growth mindset. But it is worth it for your child because believing that they increase their abilities by putting in the effort will forever change their lives for the better.

Many of the tips and tricks in this book increase your ability to help your child through whatever life throws at them. There will be a point when they struggle with something at school, in sports they play, or in life in general. Now COVID-19 has changed the way many children get educated. As a result, you and your child are now better equipped to keep a positive mindset through even the toughest of times.

Understanding how the teenage brain works gives you an advantage over other parents because you now know how to deal with the brain difference. You know how to better approach the behaviors caused by the restructuring of your teenager's brain. Once your child understands what is happening to their brain, they will make better, less risky decisions. This understanding of the brain will make them healthier and happier through the difficulties caused by puberty.

This book has given you and your child the tools to create and maintain positive and growth mindsets for many aspects of life. You even have more outside sources as well that you can pursue if you like.

I learned a great deal from writing this book, and I hope you and your child or children benefit significantly from the information I have presented.

Take this information and make your life and your child's life better.

If you find this book helpful please leave a review on Amazon.

REFERENCES

Allen, K. (n.d.). *Growth mindset toolkit.* Karen Allen. https://www.karenallen.co/toolkit

Biglifejournal.com. (2017). *How to teach growth mindset to teens.* Big Life Journal. https://biglifejournal.com/blogs/blog/teaching-teens-growth-mindset

Biglifejournal.com. (n.d.). *Kids and sports: 5 effective ways to foster a growth mindset.* Big Life Journal. https://biglifejournal.com/blogs/blog/kids-sports-growth-mindset

Cherry, K. (2020, June 3). *Overview of emotional intelligence.* Verywell Mind https://www.verywellmind.com/what-is-emotional-intelligence-2795423

Clear, J. (2013, April 11). *The Science of developing mental toughness in health, work, and life.* James Clear. https://jamesclear.com/mental-toughness

Clear, J. (2016). *Grit: A complete guide on how to be more mentally tough.* James Clear. https://jamesclear.com/grit

DeWitt, P. (2019, August 1). *A seat at the table with education week: Challenging a growth mindset in the time of covid-19.* Event.on24.com. https://event.on24.com/eventRegistration/eventRegistrationServletV2?eventid=2583888&sessionid=1&key=E58D0835A4932F764F8192469E80B656

Duckworth, A. L. (2013, April). *Grit: The power of passion and perseverance.* Www.ted.com. https://www.ted.com/talks/angela_lee_duckworth_grit_the_power_of_passion_and_perseverance?language=en#t-8985

Dweck, C. S. (2006). *Mindset: the new psychology of success.* (Updated Edition). Random House.

Gibson, C. (2020, September 28). *Molly Seidel says eating disorder remains a struggle.* Canadian Running Magazine. https://runningmagazine.ca/health-nutrition/molly-seidel-says-eating-disorder-remains-a-struggle/.

Ginsburg, K. (n.d.). Www.goodreads.com. https://www.goodreads.com/book/show/25233084-raising-kids-to-thrive

Grinberg, W. (2013, January 8). *A growth mindset is key to a culture of learning: A case study*. EJewish Philanthropy. https://ejewishphilanthropy.com/a-growth-mindset-is-key-to-a-culture-of-learning-a-case-study/

Growth Mindset Programs. (2019). Mindsetworks.com. https://www.mindsetworks.com/

Harvard Business Review. (2014, November). *How companies can profit from a "growth mindset."* https://hbr.org/2014/11/how-companies-can-profit-from-a-growth-mindset

How to change your mindset. (2016, June 14). 7 Mindsets. https://7mindsets.com/how-to-change-your-mindset/

Hunter, C. (2021, May 15). *This science-backed growth mindset strategy can boost your success in work and life*. Fast Company. https://www.fastcompany.com/90635257/this-science-backed-growth-mindset-strategy-can-boost-your-success-in-work-and-life

Loper, C. (2021, May 16). *Growth mindsets debunked? Not so fast*. Northwest Educational Services. https://www.nwtutoring.com/2021/05/16/growth-mindsets-debunked-not-so-fast/

MindsetWorks growth mindset programs. (2019). Mindsetworks.com. https://www.mindsetworks.com/

Morin, A. (2021). *6 parenting strategies for raising emotionally intelligent kids.* Verywell Family. https://www.verywellfamily.com/tips-for-raising-an-emotionally-intelligent-child-4157946

Ng, B. (2018). The neuroscience of growth mindset and intrinsic motivation. *Brain Sciences, 8*(2), 20. https://doi.org/10.3390/brainsci8020020

Paterson A. (2020, March 12). *Growth mindset and emotional intelligence.* Results through People. https://rtpeople.com.au/growth-mindset-and-emotional-intelligence/

Perlis, M. M. (2013, October 29). *5 characteristics of grit -- How many do you have?* Forbes. https://www.forbes.com/sites/margaretperlis/2013/10/29/5-characteristics-of-grit-what-it-is-why-you-need-it-and-do-you-have-it/?sh=46d866544f7b

Teacher Practices. (2012). Mindsetworks.com https://www.mindsetworks.com/Science/Teacher-Practices

The South African College of Applied Psychology (2019, September 30). *What is grit? These are the 5 characteristics.* SACAP. https://www.sacap.edu.za/blog/applied-psychology/what-is-grit/

Wheeler, S. (2016, August 23). *Can a change in mindset help teens de-stress?* Greater Good. https://greatergood.berkeley.edu/article/item/can_a_change_in_mindset_help_teens_destress#When :13:17:00Z

Zhao, H., Xiong, J., Zhang, Z., & Qi, C. (2021). Growth mindset and college students' learning engagement during the covid-19 pandemic: A serial mediation model. *Frontiers in Psychology, 12.* https://doi.org/10.3389/fpsyg.2021.621094

Printed in Great Britain
by Amazon